Ghost Sonata
AUGUST STRINDBERG

When We Dead Awaken

HENRIK IBSEN

Crofts Classics

GENERAL EDITOR
Samuel H. Beer, *Harvard University*

AUGUST STRINDBERG

Ghost Sonata

AND
HENRIK IBSEN

When We Dead Awaken

A Dramatic Epilogue
in Three Acts

Translated and Edited by
Thaddeus L. Torp
Central Connecticut State College

Harlan Davidson, Inc.
Wheeling, Illinois 60090-6000

Library of Congress Cataloging-in-Publication Data
Strindberg, August, 1849–1912.
    Ghost sonata.
    (Crofts Classics)
    Translation of: Spöksonaten / August Strindberg; and of: Når vi døde
vågner / Henrik Ibsen

    Bibliography: p. 91
    1. Scandinavian drama—Translations into English. 2. English drama—
Translations from Scandinavian. I. Torp, Thaddeus L. II. Ibsen, Henrik,
1828–l906. Når vi døde vågner. English. 1986. III. Title. IV. Title: When we
dead awaken.
[PT7092.E5S8   1986]   839.7'26'08   86-4579
ISBN 0-88295-112-2 (pbk.)

Manufactured in the United States of America
97 7 CM

contents

introduction

Henrik Ibsen, the Norwegian, and August Strindberg, his younger Swedish contemporary, have been universally accepted and acclaimed as the two writers who more than any others shaped and exemplified all that can be called modern in twentieth-century drama. And rightly so, for within the works of these two Scandinavian giants can be found classic examples of dramatic writing in which each of the main veins of contemporary theatrical art finds nurture: the well-made play of realistic preparation, the slice-of-life play of naturalistic observation, the scathing polemic comedy, the searching Freudian tragedy, the charming fantasy verse play, the contemporized historical drama, the symbolistic mystery, the expressionistic diatribe. The dramatic legacy of these two has been widely imitated, anthologized, and, most of all, produced. Rare is the repertory season without a revival of one of their plays.

The two plays in this volume represent the peculiar duality of these unique geniuses turning the formidable theatrical insight of a lifetime upon the reality of death, which both had come to confront, as indeed we all must; the plays illustrate the characteristics with which each challenged and sublimated in artistic terms this confrontation. For, whether the artist views himself as a young student confusedly stumbling into a decaying house haunted by vampires, or as a venerable sculptor tortuously climbing through bleak, sanatorium-certified air to an icy mountain peak, the antagonist is the same: Death. Not Death, the grim reaper, but Death, the sublime and wished-for release from suffering, Death, the resurrection from the earthly graveyard.

Considered primarily as thematic exercises, the plays do not fulfill all of the requirements of realistic preparation of the well-made play. Not all of their events make literal sense in a traditional chronological life span. (Try, for example, to figure out how old the young girl in *Ghost Sonata* really is! Or Irene, in *When We Dead Awaken.*) But the structural might of both plays comes from the very richness of the tapestry of symbolism with which the two are knit together. Traditional death symbols—scattered petals, wreaths, talk about funerals, old cripples, and crumbling houses—are mingled with occasional strikingly original stage pictures. In Strindberg's play the shocking entrance of the dead man in his shroud, which only the audience and the Sunday Child can react to, meets its equal in the silent progress across the stage of the woman in white with her black human shadow, which Ibsen so astutely underscores with silence. Consider, however, the unique and theatrical originality of the former's use of a milkmaid, health and youth personified, as a death-bearer; or of the latter's use of a nun, by tradition a spiritual personage, as a guardian of earthly life.

Much has been written on the musical structure of the play that Strindberg called "one of my last Sonatas." Much can be said in the same vein for Ibsen's "Epilogue." The same three-part framework exists, although Strindberg begins outside on a Sunday morning and progresses into the innermost recesses of the death house only to arrive at last in the sublime landscape of the Isle of the Dead. Ibsen, on the other hand, begins after breakfast at a fjord-level hotel and progresses up to the thin air of a mountain top and a glacial avalanche in the eternal sunlit snows. The plays seem to suggest the movement of a musical composition replete with variations and recurring leitmotif rather than division into acts and intermissions. Richard Wagner, the master of the musical leitmotif, figures in both plays: Ibsen choosing *Lohengrin*, Strindberg, *Die Walküre*. Both playwrights weld the second and third parts together with a song that then reprises at the end. And both plays make use of Maeterlinck-like silences—pauses that are written in as stage directions or inserted directly into the dialogue by means of punctuation marks as if to guide the actor the way musical notation is used to guide the musician.

Vampirism and its life-in-death qualities are, of course, more evident in *Ghost Sonata,* but the aging sculptor of *When We Dead Awaken* is accused by his victim of heartlessly stealing her soul just as Hummel is berated by the woman he has driven into the mummifying state of madness. It is in these twin figures—the two women who posed for nude statues and married without love, insane living corpses yearning to die and escape the grave they see life to be and who in the age-old tradition of stage madness speak only lucid truth—that the two plays find their most obvious outward similarity, and, at the same time, reflect most clearly the individualizing traits of their creators.

The theater supplies an imagery that only production can truly bring forth. I am certain, however, that any reader venturing into the fantastic scenery presupposed by the minds of these two production-wise craftsmen of the practical stage and listening with the stage-oriented ears of these two trained practitioners will come away enchanted. That enchantment is the spell that only great theater can weave.

notes on the translation

The translation of *Ghost Sonata* was prepared, as has been my practice, for college production. In so doing I became particularly aware of the typography of the Swedish edition in contrast to that of most English-language versions, the most obvious being that the play is written as one continuous action, as is *Miss Julie,* and not broken into separate scenes or acts, as most translators have insisted. The Swedish edition is broken at irregular intervals by open lines with the insertion

(Paus.)

after which the dialogue continues. Or at times the more usual practice of a single asterisk

*

seems to set apart two French scenes, because it is either preceded by an exit or followed by an entrance. In the English versions available to me, the pauses are inserted parenthetically in the running dialogue—(Pause)—which deprives them of dramatic weight and equates them with similarly included instructions to the actors. The asterisks are in most cases not even retained in the English adaptations.

Ibsen's play, more conventional in typography in the Gyldendal edition, is divided into acts and makes use of pauses and silences only in the traditional manner of parenthetic insertion within speeches.

Internal punctuation within dialogue was also of interest to me in preparing the text for production. Strindberg, I found, has used two devices: a dash and a series of dots or periods, usually three in number. This causes a speech such as the Old Man's to Johansson to look like this:

> GUBBEN. Jasa inte hemma? Du ar et fa! — Ock telegrafen? — Ingenting . . . Vidare! . . . Klockan 6 i aften? Det ar bra! — Extranumerat? — Hela namnet ute! Student Arkenholz, fodd . . . foraldrar . . . utmarkt . . . jag tror det borjar regna . . .

In order to understand the playwright's mind, I wished as a director to adhere to this clearly differentiated dramatic shorthand. My translation, therefore, duplicates this typography accurately.

Ibsen uses the dash, and he uses it here with more elaborations than in any of his earlier plays.

As for the language itself, I have tried to resist what so often amounts to poetic license with words. Strindberg's Swedish is direct almost to obtuseness at times. I set out to use the most direct American equivalencies and avoid the Britishisms present in most of the translations. Take the obvious example of the Young Lady's reply to the student when he asks her about the cook.

> STUDENTEN. Vem ar denna jattekvinna?
> FROKEN. Hon tillfor vampirfamiljen Hummel; hon ater opp oss . . .

Paulson translates:

> STUDENT. Who is this Gargantuan bulk of a woman?
> YOUNG LADY. She belongs to the Hummel family of vampires. She is devouring us alive . . .

"Gargantuan bulk of a woman" is unnecessary poeticizing
for "jattekvinna." One simple word, "giantess" or "ogress,"
is all the playwright wants his actor to cry out. And the reply
should be as direct. "Belongs to" I do not quibble with—but
the suspense of the line is the name Hummel—it must have
the weight Strindberg intended, following and not preced-
ing the vampire designation. And "devouring us alive . . ."?
Why not the most direct, most shocking, even if ungram-
matical (would a real Swedish lady in proper parlor fiction
use such a vulgar, monosyllabic phrase?): "She is eating us
up . . ."? I can attest to the force of that line on the stage,
and any actress will find it easier to say than "devouring us
alive . . ." for all its poetry and added connotative value.

Ibsen's language is a peculiar mixture of realistic prose
and elevated prose-verse. I experienced difficulties at the
beginning of each act and soon discovered that this was
where Ibsen had his greatest difficulties, because each act
opens with Maia, who speaks a difficult, almost Strindber-
gian prose. When Irene enters to converse with Rubek, the
language thins out and the echo-like effect of the words can
be felt so plainly it was a necessity that this carry over into
the English translation.

Thus, the tongues of actors and the ear of the director
have tempered this attempt to bring two works of genius to
a wider audience.

chronology of important

Ibsen

events and principal works

Strindberg

1849	Born: Stockholm, Sweden, January 22
1862	Death of his mother
1867	Student at Uppsala University
1869	Student at Royal Academy of Acting
1870	First published play: *The Free Thinker; In Rome* performed at Royal Theater
1877	Marriage to Siri von Essen
1879	*The Red Room* (a novel): first literary success
1881	*Master Olof:* successful in performance

1882	*An Enemy of the People:* Contrary to practice, took only one year to write this
1884	*The Wild Duck*
1886	*Rosmersholm*
1888	*The Lady from the Sea*
1890	*Hedda Gabler*
1891	Returns to Oslo, Norway
1892	*The Master Builder*
1894	*Little Eyolf*
1896	*John Gabriel Borkman*
1898	No play; 70th birthday caused celebrations and revivals
1899	*When We Dead Awaken:* the last play
1900	Deteriorating health
1901	Paralyzed by a stroke
1906	Died May 23, Oslo, Norway

1882	*Lucky Per's Journey*
1883	Strindberg leaves Scandinavia
1884	The play *Married;* unsuccessfully prosecuted for blasphemy
1886	Autobiography (four volumes)
1887	*The Father; Comrades;* plans for an Experimental Theater in Denmark
1888	*Miss Julie; Creditors*
1891	Divorced Siri
1892	*The Bond; Motherlove; Playing with Fire*
1893	Marriage to Frida Uhl
1894	Separated; beginning of Inferno crisis
1896	Return to Sweden at Lund
1897	*Inferno;* Divorce from Frida
1898	*To Damascus I & II;* copy sent to Ibsen
1899	*Crimes and Crimes; Gustav Vasa;* and historical plays; return to Stockholm
1900	*Dance of Death; Easter;* a greatly productive year
1901	Married to Harriet Bosse; *Swanwhite; Queen Christina; To Damascus III*
1902	Separated; *A Dream Play; Gustav III*
1904	Divorced Harriet
1906	Historical prose; last volume of autobiography
1907	Founding of Intimate Theater; wrote the Chamber Plays (incl. *Ghost Sonata*)
1909	*The Great Highway:* the last play
1912	Died May 14 of cancer in Stockholm

Neither author received the Nobel Prize. For events and dates, I am primarily indebted to F. L. Lucas, *The Drama of Ibsen and Strindberg,* 1962.

Ghost Sonata

AUGUST STRINDBERG

Translated from the Swedish by
Thaddeus L. Torp

CHARACTERS

OLD MAN
STUDENT, *Arkenholz*
MILKMAID *(a vision)*
JANITRESS
JANITOR *(Doorman)*[1]
DEAD MAN, *a Consul*
THE DARK LADY, *daughter of the* JANITRESS *by the* DEAD MAN
COLONEL
MUMMY, *the* COLONEL*'s wife*
HIS DAUGHTER, *The Young Lady, really the* OLD MAN*'s daughter*
THE ARISTOCRAT, *called Baron Skanskorg. Engaged to the* JANITRESS*'s daughter*
JOHANSSON, *the servant of* HUMMEL
BENGTSSON, *employed by the* COLONEL
FIANCÉE, HUMMEL*'s former fiancée, a white-haired old lady* Cook, Maidservant, Beggars[2]

(The ground floor and one upper story of the façade of a modern house. The house terminates to the right with a round room on the ground floor, above which, on the upper story, are a balcony and a flag-stand.
Through the open windows of this round salon, with its sun-blinds drawn up, can be seen a white marble statue of a young woman surrounded by palms and starkly lighted by the sun's rays. In the windows to the left are many pots of hyacinths (blue, white, pink).
On the balcony railing in the corner above are a blue silk comforter and two white pillows. The windows to the left are hung with white sheets. It is a clear Sunday morning.
In front of the house in the foreground stands a green bench.

[1]This character is listed by the author in the cast but does not appear in the script.
[2]These are not listed in the cast, but do appear.

To the right in the foreground, a street fountain; to the left, an advertising column.

To the left through the open entrance door can be seen a staircase, with steps of white marble, and a railing of mahogany and brass. At both sides of the door on the pavement stand laurels in tubs.

The corner with the round room also faces a side street, which runs upstage.

To the left of the entrance door on the main floor is a window with a reflecting glass.

With the rising of the curtain, the bells of several churches can be heard ringing in the distance.

The doors of the house are open; a darkly clad woman stands motionless on the staircase.

The JANITRESS is sweeping the stoop; then she polishes the brass on the door; then she waters her laurels.

In a wheelchair by the column the OLD MAN sits and reads the newspaper; he has white hair and beard and wears glasses.

The MILKMAID comes in from the right with bottles in a wire basket; she wears a summer dress, with brown shoes, black stockings, and a white cap; she takes off the cap and hangs it on the fountain; wipes the sweat from her brow; drinks from the dipper; washes her hands; puts her hair in order, using the water as a looking glass.

A steamship's bell rings, and now and then the silence is pierced by the low notes of an organ in a church nearby.

After a few minutes' silence, when the MILKMAID has finished her toilet, the STUDENT comes in from the left, sleepless, unshaven. He goes straight to the fountain.)

(*Pause*)

STUDENT. May I use the dipper?

MILKMAID. (*Hugs the dipper to herself.*)

STUDENT. Haven't you finished yet?

MILKMAID. (*Stares at him in terror.*)

OLD MAN. (*To himself*) Who is he talking with? — I see nothing! — Is he crazy?

STUDENT. What are you staring at? Do I look terrible? Yes, I haven't slept all night, and naturally you think that I've been out boozing . . .

MILKMAID. *(Remains the same.)*

STUDENT. Drinking punch, huh? Do I smell like punch?

MILKMAID. *(Remains the same.)*

STUDENT. I haven't shaven, I know that. . . . Give me a drink of water, I've earned it. *(Pause)* No? Then I must tell you. I bandaged wounds and worked over sick people for the whole night. You see, I was there when the house collapsed yesterday evening. . . . Now you know.

MILKMAID. *(Rinses the dipper and offers him a drink.)*

STUDENT. Thanks!

MILKMAID. *(Unmovable)*

STUDENT. *(Slowly)* Will you do me a big favor? *(Pause)* It's like this, my eyes are inflamed, as you can see—but my hands have touched wounds and the like—so—I cannot put them near my eyes. . . . Will you take my clean handkerchief, soak it in that fresh water, and bathe my sore eyes with it? Will you do that?—Will you be the Good Samaritan?

MILKMAID. *(Hesitates, but does as he asks.)*

STUDENT. Thanks, Friend! *(He takes out his wallet.)*

MILKMAID. *(Makes gesture of refusal.)*

STUDENT. I'm sorry. Forgive my thoughtlessness. I'm not really awake. . . .

OLD MAN. *(To the* STUDENT*)* Excuse me, but I heard you were there, at the catastrophe yesterday evening. . . . I have been sitting here reading about it in the paper. . . .

STUDENT. Is it already in there?

OLD MAN. Yes, the whole thing! And your picture is with it. But they regret that they were unable to find out the brave young student's name. . . .

STUDENT. *(Looking at paper)* Yes, that is me! What do you know!

OLD MAN. Who was that you were talking to just now?

STUDENT. Didn't you see?

(Pause)

OLD MAN. Is it nosy to ask — to get from you — your real name?

STUDENT. What would that serve? I don't think of publicity. — If one is praised then criticism follows. — The art of running people down has been built up to such a height —besides, I don't ask for any reward. . . .

OLD MAN. Wealthy perhaps?

STUDENT. Not at all . . . the opposite! I'm broke.

OLD MAN. Here now . . . I think I've heard your voice before. . . . When I was young I had a friend who couldn't pronounce window; he always said "winder." — I've never met one person who said it that way but him. — Is it possible that you are related to the merchandiser Arkenholz?

STUDENT. That was my father.

OLD MAN. The ways of fate are strange. . . . I remember you as a baby, under very painful conditions. . . .

STUDENT. Yes, I learned I was born into the world in the middle of bankruptcy proceedings. . . .

OLD MAN. Ah yes!

STUDENT. Might I ask your name?

OLD MAN. I am Director Hummel.

STUDENT. You are the . . . ? I remember that . . .

OLD MAN. You've heard my name often spoken in your family?

STUDENT. Yes.

OLD MAN. And spoken with good will?

STUDENT. *(Remains silent.)*

OLD MAN. Yes, I can well imagine! — They said to you that I was the man who ruined your father—all who ruin themselves through speculations find the cause for their ruin in those they couldn't fool. *(Pause)* The truth of the matter is that your father stripped me of seventeen thousand crowns, the whole of my savings at the time.

STUDENT. It's strange how the same story can be told in two so opposite ways.

OLD MAN. You surely don't think I've been telling lies?

STUDENT. What should I think? My father didn't lie.

OLD MAN. That's true, a father never lies . . . but I am also a father, and so it follows . . .

STUDENT. What are you coming to?

OLD MAN. I saved your father from misery, and he repaid me with all the hatred that a man feels when he is obligated to be grateful. . . . He taught his family to speak ill of me.

STUDENT. Perhaps you made him ungrateful by giving help with unnecessary humiliations.

OLD MAN. All help is humiliating, sir.

STUDENT. What do you want of me?

OLD MAN. I am not seeking money. But if you would do me a small service, then I would consider myself repaid. Now, you see that I am crippled—some say it's my own fault —others blame my parents—I think myself that it is life itself that is to blame; in avoiding one of its traps you fall right into the next one. Anyway, I can't run up and down stairs, can't even ring bell cords. For that reason I ask you: Help me!

STUDENT. What can I do?

OLD MAN. First of all you might give my chair a push so that I can look at those posters. I want to see what's playing this evening.

STUDENT. *(Pushing the wheelchair)* Have you no man with you?

OLD MAN. Yes, but he's off on an errand . . . coming right back . . . are you a medical student?

STUDENT. No, I'm studying languages. But I don't know what I want to be . . .

OLD MAN. Ho, ho! — How's your mathematics?

STUDENT. Yes, not bad.

OLD MAN. That is good! So we can reach an arrangement, perhaps?

STUDENT. Yes, why not?

OLD MAN. Great! *(Reading the posters)* They're doing *Die Walküre* for the matinee. . . . So the Colonel will be there with his daughter. And since he always sits on the aisle in the sixth row, I'll put you in the next seat. . . . Will you go into the telephone booth over there and order a ticket for seat number eighty-two in the sixth row?

STUDENT. Shall I go to the opera in the afternoon?

OLD MAN. Yes! And if you let me guide you, then you won't regret it. I want you to be happy, rich, and respected. Your debut last night as the brave rescuer will make you well known tomorrow, and your name will be worth much.

STUDENT. *(Going toward the telephone booth)* What an amusing adventure.

OLD MAN. Are you a sportsman?

STUDENT. Yes, that is my misfortune . . .

OLD MAN. Then we shall call it fortune! — Now go and telephone!

(He picks up his newspaper and starts to read.)

(The DARK LADY *has come out on the sidewalk to talk with the* JANITRESS. *The* OLD MAN *listens, but the audience hears nothing.)*

STUDENT. *(Comes in again.)*

OLD MAN. Did you do it?

STUDENT. Yes I did.

OLD MAN. Do you see that house?

STUDENT. Yes I've been observing it . . . I walked by here yesterday, when the sun was shining on the window panes —and I thought of all the beauty and luxury that one would find inside—I said to my friend, "Think of living there, four flights up, a beautiful wife, two pretty kids, and twenty thousand crowns in income . . ."

OLD MAN. So you said? So you said? Well now! I also am very fond of that house . . .

STUDENT. Do you speculate in houses?

OLD MAN. Mmm—yes! But not in the way you mean . . .

STUDENT. Do you know those who live there?

OLD MAN. All. When one gets to be as old as I am, one knows everybody, their fathers and their forefathers—and you always find you are related to them somehow—I am now eighty—But no one knows me, really. — I interest myself in the fate of mankind . . .

(The curtains in the round room are drawn. The COLONEL *is seen inside, dressed in civilian clothes. After having looked at the thermometer, he goes back into the room and stands in front of the marble statue.)*

OLD MAN. See, there is the Colonel! Whom you will sit next to this afternoon . . .

STUDENT. Is that—the Colonel? I don't understand any of this. It's like a story . . .

OLD MAN. The whole of my life is like something in a storybook, sir. But although the stories are different, one thread ties them all together and the same leitmotif recurs constantly.

STUDENT. Who is that marble statue there?

OLD MAN. That's his wife, naturally . . .

STUDENT. Was she so wonderful?

OLD MAN. Ah yes . . . yes.

STUDENT. Tell me!

OLD MAN. We can't judge other human beings, dear boy! —And if I were to tell you that she left him, that he beat her, that she came back again and married him again, and that *she* now sits in there like a mummy, and worships her own statue, then would you think I was crazy?

STUDENT. I don't get it!

OLD MAN. I didn't think you would!—Then we have the hyacinth window. That's where his daughter lives . . . She's out horseback riding, but she'll be home soon . . .

STUDENT. Who is the dark lady who is talking to the caretaker's wife?

OLD MAN. Yes, this is a bit complicated . . . But it's associated with the dead man up there, where you see the white sheets . . .

STUDENT. Why, who is he?

OLD MAN. He was a human being, like us. But he was noted for his vanity . . . Now if you were a Sunday child, you would soon see him come out of that door just to check the Consulate flag at half-mast. — His title was Consul. He loved lions, plumed hats, and colored ribbons.

STUDENT. You spoke of a Sunday child. — I was born on a Sunday.

OLD MAN. No, were you? . . . I might have known . . . I see it from the color of your eyes . . . then you can see what others can't see, haven't you noticed that?

STUDENT. I don't know what others see. But sometimes . . . Well, one doesn't tell such things!

OLD MAN. I was almost certain of that! But you can tell me . . . because I—understand such things . . .

STUDENT. For example, yesterday . . . I was drawn to that unfamiliar street where the house was to collapse . . . I walked down the street and stood in front of a building that I had never seen before . . . then I noticed a crack in the wall. I could hear the cross beams cracking, I leaped forward and clutched a child that was under the wall . . . In the next second the house collapsed . . . I was safe, but in my arms where I thought I held the child, nothing . . .

OLD MAN. That's quite a story . . . I thought as much . . . but tell me something: why were you making all those gestures just now at the fountain? And why were you talking to yourself?

STUDENT. Didn't you see the milkmaid I was speaking with?

OLD MAN. *(Terrified)* Milkmaid?

STUDENT. Of course. She gave me the dipper.

OLD MAN. Yes, hmm? So that's how things sit ... Well now, I may not have seen, but I can do other ...

(A white-haired woman sits down at the window with the reflecting glass.)

OLD MAN. See that old woman in the window! Do you see her? ... Good! That was my fiancée—once, sixty years ago ... I was twenty. — Don't worry, she doesn't know me. We see each other every day, but it doesn't have the least effect on me, although we swore to love each other forever! Forever!

STUDENT. How foolish you were in those days! We never tell such things to our girls.

OLD MAN. Forgive us, young man. We didn't know any better—but can you see that that old woman was once young and beautiful?

STUDENT. It doesn't show. Well, maybe. She has a lovely way of looking at things ... I can't see her eyes.

JANITRESS. *(Comes out with a basket and spreads greenery on the sidewalk.)*

OLD MAN. Aha, the janitress! — That dark lady is her daughter by the dead man upstairs. That's why her husband got the job as caretaker ... But the dark lady has a fiancé, he is an aristocrat and expects to be rich. He's getting a divorce from his present wife, who is giving him a stone house just to get rid of him. The aristocratic lover is a son-in-law of the dead man, and you see his night clothes being aired on the balcony up there ... This is complicated, you can see!

STUDENT. It's terribly complicated!

OLD MAN. Yes, that it is, inside and out, although at first it looks simple.

STUDENT. But who was the dead man there?

OLD MAN. You just asked me and I told you. If you look around the corner where the servants' entrance is, you'll see all of the poor people whom he helped ... when he felt like it ...

STUDENT. He was a charitable man then?

OLD MAN. Yes ... sometimes.

STUDENT. Not always?

OLD MAN. No! ... Such is the way of mankind. — Here

now, sir, push my chair so I am in the sun. I'm freezing cold. When you never get to move around, the blood stops. — I will die soon, I know that. But first I have some things to do. — Take my hand, just feel how cold I am.

STUDENT. That's not possible! *(Rigidly)*

OLD MAN. Don't leave me; I'm tired and I'm lonely, but I haven't always been this way. I have an infinitely long life behind me—infinitely—I've made people unhappy and people have made me unhappy, the one cancels the other. — But before I die I want to see you happy . . . our fates are bound together because of your father and other things . . .

STUDENT. Let go of my hand; you are drawing my strength from me—you are freezing me, what do you want of me?

OLD MAN. Be patient. You will see and understand . . . there comes the young lady . . .

STUDENT. The Colonel's daughter?

OLD MAN. Yes! *His* daughter! Look at her! — Have you ever seen such a masterpiece?

STUDENT. She looks like the marble statue in there . . .

OLD MAN. That is of her mother!

STUDENT. You're right! — Never have I seen such a woman of women born. — Fortunate is the man who will lead her from the altar to his home!

OLD MAN. Yes, you can see that! — Not everyone recognized her beauty . . . So, it is written!

*

(YOUNG LADY enters from the left dressed in a riding habit, in the manner of a modern English Amazon, and crosses slowly without looking at anyone, over to the door of the house. There she stops and says a few words to the JANITRESS. Then she enters the house.)

STUDENT. *(Covers his eyes with his hands.)*

OLD MAN. Are you crying?

STUDENT. In the face of what is hopeless, what can I do but despair?

OLD MAN. I can open doors and hearts; if only I can find an arm to do my will . . . Serve me, and you will have power . . .

STUDENT. Is this a pact? Shall I sell my soul?

OLD MAN. Sell nothing! — Listen, I have *taken* all my life! Now I have a longing to give! to give! But, no one will take from me . . . I'm rich, very rich, but I have no heirs. Oh, yes, one bum who torments the life out of me . . . Be a son to me, become my heir, enjoy life while I am here to see it, if only from a distance.

STUDENT. What must I do?

OLD MAN. Go and hear *Die Walküre* first!

STUDENT. That I have already agreed to. — What more?

OLD MAN. This evening you shall be sitting in there in the round salon!

STUDENT. How shall I get in there?

OLD MAN. By way of *Die Walküre*!

STUDENT. Why have you chosen me for your medium? Did you know me before?

OLD MAN. Yes, naturally! I've had my eyes on you for a long time . . . But now there, see on the balcony, the maid is raising the flag to half-mast for the Consul . . . and now she is turning over the bed clothes . . . do you see that blue quilt? — It was made for two to sleep under, but now it is for one . . .

(YOUNG LADY, in a change of clothes, waters the hyacinths in the window.)

OLD MAN. There's my little girl. Look at her, look! — She's talking to the flowers now. Is she not herself like a blue hyacinth? . . . She gives them drink, nothing but water, and they change the water into color and fragrance . . . Now, here comes the Colonel with the newspaper — He's showing her the collapsed house . . . Now he's pointing to your picture! She's interested . . . She's reading about your bravery . . . It appears to be clouding over. Suppose it starts to rain? I'm sitting pretty here if Johansson doesn't come back soon . . .

(It grows cloudy and dark. The old woman at the window mirror closes her window.)

OLD MAN. Now my fiancée is closing her window . . . seventy-nine years . . . that window mirror is the only mirror she ever uses. That's because she can't see herself, only the outside world and that in two directions. But the world can see her. She doesn't realize that . . . all the same, a handsome old woman.

(*Now the* DEAD MAN *in a shroud comes out of the main door.*)

STUDENT. Good lord, what do I see?

OLD MAN. What do you see?

STUDENT. Don't *you* see, in the doorway, a dead man?

OLD MAN. I see nothing. But I expected something like this. Tell me . . .

STUDENT. He's stepping out into the street . . .

(*Pause*)

Now he's turning his head and looking up at the flag.

OLD MAN. What did I tell you? He has come out to count the floral offerings and read each calling card . . . Woe to those who forgot!

STUDENT. Now he's going to the corner . . .

OLD MAN. He will check the poor people at the servants' entrance . . . The poor people decorate a death house so well: "Received in death the blessings of the populace!" Yes, but no blessings from me! — between us, he was a great scoundrel . . .

STUDENT. But charitable . . .

OLD MAN. A charitable scoundrel, who thought only of a glorious funeral . . . When he could feel his end was near, he embezzled from the state, fifty-thousand crowns . . . Now his daughter is living with another woman's husband and worrying about his will . . . He can hear every word we're saying, the scoundrel, and that will serve him right! — Here comes Johansson!

JOHANSSON. (*Enters from the left.*)

OLD MAN. Report!

JOHANSSON. (*Talks inaudibly.*)

OLD MAN. Not at home? You're a fool! — And the telegram? — nothing! . . . Go on! . . . Six o'clock this evening? That's good! — A special edition? — With his full name? — Arkenholz, student—born . . . parents . . . excellent . . . I think it's beginning to rain. . . . What did he say? . . . I see!

... He will not? — Well, he must! — Here comes the Aristocrat! — Push me around the corner, Johansson, I want to hear what the poor people are saying ... And, Arkenholz: Wait for me here ... Do you understand? — Hurry up, hurry up!

JOHANSSON. *(Pushes the wheelchair around the corner.)*

STUDENT. *(Remains and admires the young lady who is raking the earth in the flower pots.)*

*

ARISTOCRAT. *(Dressed in mourning, enters and speaks to the* DARK LADY, *who comes out onto the sidewalk.)* Yes, what can one do about it? — We must wait!

DARK LADY. But I can't wait!

ARISTOCRAT. Is that so? Go to the country then!

DARK LADY. I will not do that!

ARISTOCRAT. Come over here. Someone will hear what we're saying.

(They go over toward the advertisement column and continue their conversation inaudibly.)

JOHANSSON. *(Enters from the right. To the* STUDENT*)* The master bids you, sir, not to forget the other matter—!

STUDENT. *(Slowly)* Here now,—tell me first, who is the master?

JOHANSSON. Yes! He's so many things, and he's been everything.

STUDENT. Is he sane?

JOHANSSON. Well, what is that? — He has all of his life sought after a Sunday child, so he says. But that might not be true ...

STUDENT. What is he after? Does he want wealth?

JOHANSSON. He wants power ... The whole day he rides around in his chariot like the god Thor ... He looks at houses, tears them down, opens up streets, rebuilds shopping centers. But he also breaks into houses, creeps in through the windows, toys with human fates, kills his enemies, and never forgives — Yes, can you imagine, sir, that that little cripple was once a Don Juan? But he always lost his woman.

STUDENT. How can you account for that?

JOHANSSON. Well, he is so cunning that he knew how to get his women to leave when he got tired of them . . . But that was a long time ago. Nowadays he's more like a horse thief at a human market. He steals human beings, of all sorts . . . Myself, he literally stole out of the hands of justice . . . I had made a little blunder—hmm; and only he knew about it. But instead of putting me in jail, he made me his slave. I slave for my meat—which is far from the best . . .

STUDENT. What's he want to do with this house?

JOHANSSON. Well, that I wouldn't want to say. It is very complicated.

STUDENT. I think I'd best get out of here . . .

JOHANSSON. See, the young lady has dropped her bracelet out of the window . . .

(The YOUNG LADY *drops her bracelet out of the open window.)*

STUDENT. *(Crosses over, picks up the bracelet, and hands it to the* YOUNG LADY, *who thanks him stiffly. The* STUDENT *goes back to* JOHANSSON.*)*

JOHANSSON. Ah yes, so you're thinking of going . . . It isn't as easy as you think once he has slipped his net over your head . . . and he dreads nothing between heaven and earth . . . Yes, one thing, or rather one person . . .

STUDENT. Wait now, perhaps I know!

JOHANSSON. How can you know?

STUDENT. I can guess!—Is it . . . a little milkmaid he dreads?

JOHANSSON. He turns his face away whenever he sees a milk wagon . . . and he talks in his sleep. He was once somewhere in Hamburg . . .

STUDENT. Can one trust that man?

JOHANSSON. One can trust him—He'll do anything!

STUDENT. What is he doing around the corner now?

JOHANSSON. He's listening to the beggars . . . planting a little word, plucking out a grain of sand, until the whole house collapses . . . figuratively speaking . . . Oh yes, I am a well-read man and I used to be a bookseller . . . Are you going now?

STUDENT. I don't want to seem ungrateful . . . That man aided my father once, and now all he's asking is a little favor in return . . .

JOHANSSON. What is that?

STUDENT. I will go and see *Die Walküre* . . .

JOHANSSON. I don't understand that . . . he's up to something new . . . see now, he's talking to the policeman . . . He's always involved with the police. He makes use of them, involves them in his business, binds them with false promises and expectations. And all the while he's pumping them. — You shall see, before the night is over they'll be receiving him in that round salon.

STUDENT. What does he want in there? What's between him and the Colonel?

JOHANSSON. Well . . . I could guess but I won't! You'll see for yourself when you go there . . .

STUDENT. I'll never come to be there . . .

JOHANSSON. That depends on you! — Go to *Die Walküre*!

STUDENT. Is that the way?

JOHANSSON. Yes, if he said so! — Look at him, just look at him! Riding his war chariot, drawn in triumph by the beggars who don't get a cent for it, just a hint that something might come their way at his funeral!

OLD MAN. *(Enters standing in his wheelchair, drawn by one of the beggars, and followed by the others.)* Hail the noble youth, who at the risk of his own life saved many lives in yesterday's catastrophe! Hail, Arkenholz!

BEGGARS. *(Bare their heads but do not cheer.)*

YOUNG LADY. *(Waves her handkerchief from the window.)*

COLONEL. *(Stares out through the window.)*

FIANCÉE. *(Stands up at her window.)*

MAID. *(On the balcony raises the flag to the top.)*

OLD MAN. Clap your hands, my fellow citizens! I know that it is Sunday, but the ass toiling at the well and the ear growing in the field grant us absolution. Though I am not a Sunday child, I have the gift of prophecy and healing. I once called a drowning girl back to life . . . yes, it was in Hamburg, on a Sunday, like this one . . .

*

MILKMAID. *(Enters, seen only by the STUDENT and the OLD MAN; she stretches her arms up like a drowning person and stares fixedly at the OLD MAN.)*

OLD MAN. *(Sits down, and shrinks within himself in terror.)*
Johansson, take me away! Quickly! — Arkenholz, don't forget *Die Walküre!*

STUDENT. What is all this?

JOHANSSON. We shall see! We shall see!

*

*(In the round salon. In the back a white glazed stove with
pendulums and a candelabra. To the right is a hall with a view
into a green room with mahogany furniture. To the left stands
the statue shadowed by palms and curtains that can be drawn
around it. To the left in the rear is the door to the hyacinth
room, there the* YOUNG LADY *sits and reads. The* COLONEL's
*back can be seen from where he sits and writes in the green
room.*

BENGTSSON, *the servant, wearing livery, enters from the hall
with* JOHANSSON *in a frock coat and a white tie.)*

BENGTSSON. Now, you, Johansson, shall serve while I take
care of the coats. Have you done this kind of thing before?

JOHANSSON. You know, I push that war chariot all day, but
in the evenings I sometimes serve at parties. It's always been
my dream to come into this house . . . they're strange people, aren't they?

BENGTSSON. Yes, a bit unusual one might say.

JOHANSSON. Is this a musical evening? Or what is the
occasion?

BENGTSSON. It is the usual ghost supper, as we call it.
They drink tea, saying not a word, unless the Colonel talks
by himself: and so they nibble their crackers all in unison.
They sound like a pack of rats in the attic.

JOHANSSON. Why do you call it a ghost supper?

BENGTSSON. Well, they look like ghosts . . . this has been
going on for twenty years—always the same people, saying
the same things, or else keeping silent for fear of saying
something embarrassing.

JOHANSSON. Where's the wife in this house?

BENGTSSON. Oh, yes. She's crazy, sits in a clothes closet
because her eyes can't take the light . . . She's sitting in there
. . . *(He points to a door in the wall that's covered with wallpaper.)*

JOHANSSON. In there?

BENGTSSON. Yes, I told you they were a little bit unusual . . .

JOHANSSON. What does she look like?

BENGTSSON. Like a mummy . . . Would you like to see? *(He opens the papered door.)* There she sits!

JOHANSSON. Body of Christ . . .

*

MUMMY. *(Jabbering)* Why do you open the door? Haven't I said it must be kept closed? . . .

BENGTSSON. *(Mimicking her jabber)* Ta, ta, ta, ta! Little baby must be good now, if she wants to get a treat—Pretty Polly!

MUMMY. *(Like a parrot)* Pretty Polly! Is Jacob there? Kurrrrre!

BENGTSSON. She thinks she's a parrot, and maybe she is . . . *(To the* MUMMY*)* Polly, whistle a little for us!

MUMMY. *(Whistles.)*

JOHANSSON. I have seen a lot, but nothing like this!

BENGTSSON. Well, you see, when a house gets old, it starts to decay, and when people sit together for a long time and torment each other too long, they go nutty. The woman of this house—shush, Polly! — This mummy has been sitting here for forty years—same husband, same furniture, same relatives, same friends . . . *(Closes the door on the* MUMMY*.)* And what has passed in this house—of that I know little . . . look at this statue here . . . that's the woman when young!

JOHANSSON. Good lord! — Is this the mummy?

BENGTSSON. Yes!—it's enough to make you weak! — But this woman because of her imagination or something has taken to parroting behavior! — She can't tolerate the crippled and the sick . . . she can't even tolerate her own daughter because she's sick . . .

JOHANSSON. Is the young girl sick?

BENGTSSON. Didn't you know that?

JOHANSSON. No! . . . And the Colonel? Who is he?

BENGTSSON. That you shall see!

JOHANSSON. *(Looking at the statue)* It's heartwringing to think of that . . . How old is the woman now?

BENGTSSON. That no one knows ... but it is told that when she was thirty-five she looked like nineteen, and she got the Colonel to imagine that she was ... here in this house ... Do you know what that black Japanese screen is for by the chaise longue? — They call it death's screen, and stand it in front when someone is dying, the same as in the hospital.

JOHANSSON. This is a horrible house ... and for it the student has been longing as one does for paradise ...

BENGTSSON. Which student? Oh yes, him! The one who is coming here this evening ... The Colonel and the young lady met him at the opera and were very taken with him ... Hmmm! ... But now it is my turn to ask a question: Who is his patron? The director in the wheelchair ... ?

JOHANSSON. Yes, yes! Is he coming here also?

BENGTSSON. He has not been invited.

JOHANSSON. Then he'll come uninvited! If need be ...

*

OLD MAN. *(Appears in the hall, in frock coat and top hat, on crutches. He sneaks forward and listens.)*

BENGTSSON. That's a regular old thief, right?

JOHANSSON. Absolutely!

BENGTSSON. He looks like the devil himself!

JOHANSSON. He must also be a sorceror—because, he can go through locked doors ...

OLD MAN. *(Coming forward, and taking* JOHANSSON *by the ear)* Crook! — Take care! *(To* BENGTSSON*)* Announce me at once to the Colonel!

BENGTSSON. Yes, but he expects guests ...

OLD MAN. That I know! But my visit he half-expects, though it's not looked forward to ...

BENGTSSON. Ah so! And the name! Director Hummel!

OLD MAN. Exactly so!

BENGTSSON. *(Goes down the hall into the green room, where he closes the door.)*

OLD MAN. *(To* JOHANSSON*)* Get out!

JOHANSSON. *(Hesitates.)*

OLD MAN. Get out!

JOHANSSON. *(Vanishes down the hall.)*

OLD MAN. *(Inspects the room. Stands before the statue in great amazement.)*

Amalia! . . . It is she! . . . She! *(He roams about the room fingering everything, puts his wig in order in front of the mirror. Returns to the statue.)*

MUMMY. *(Inside the closet.)* Pretty Polly!

OLD MAN. *(Startled)* What was that! Is there a parrot in the room? But I see nothing!

MUMMY. Is Jacob there?

OLD MAN. A spook!

MUMMY. Jacob!

OLD MAN. Where are my wits? . . . It is such secrets they've been keeping in this house! *(He studies a portrait with his back to the closet.)* That is him . . . him!

MUMMY. *(Comes forward behind the old man and pulls his wig.)* Kurrre! Is it you, Kurrr-e?

OLD MAN. *(Jumps in the air.)* Oh my God in heaven! — Who is this?

MUMMY. *(Speaking with a human voice)* Aren't you Jacob?

OLD MAN. I am called Jacob, surname . . .

MUMMY. *(With emotion)* And I am called Amalia!

OLD MAN. No, No, No, . . . Jesus Christ . . .

MUMMY. So I look, now! Yes! — And I used to look like *that*! That is what life has done to me. — I live mostly in a closet, not only to avoid seeing, but to avoid being seen . . . but you, Jacob, what are you seeking here?

OLD MAN. My child! Our child . . .

MUMMY. She's sitting in there.

OLD MAN. Where?

MUMMY. There, in the hyacinth room.

OLD MAN. *(Looking at the* YOUNG LADY*)* Yes, that is she!

(Pause)

What does her father say, I mean the Colonel? Your husband?

MUMMY. I was angry with him once, and told him everything . . .

OLD MAN. No-o?

MUMMY. He didn't believe me. He only said, "That's what all wives say when they want to murder their husbands." — It was a brutal thing to do. His whole life is a lie, even his family tree. When I look at the list of nobility, and think to myself: She has a false birth certificate, like a commoner. For such things people go to prison.

OLD MAN. There are many who do that. You once told me that you were born . . .

MUMMY. That was my mother, she made me . . . don't blame me! . . . But you had as much as I to do with the crime we committed.

OLD MAN. No! Your husband was to blame for that, he stole my fiancée from me! — I was born so that I can never forgive until I have punished. — I took that as an inevitable duty . . . I still do so!

MUMMY. What are you seeking in this house? What do you want? And how did you get in? — Is it about my daughter? If you touch her, you shall die!

OLD MAN. I only wish her well!

MUMMY. Then you must spare her father!

OLD MAN. No!

MUMMY. Then you shall die; in this room; behind that screen . . .

OLD MAN. Maybe . . . but I can't let loose once I sink my teeth in . . .

MUMMY. You wish to marry her to that student. Why? He has nothing and is nothing.

OLD MAN. He will be rich, because of me!

MUMMY. Were you invited here this evening?

OLD MAN. No, but I've decided to invite myself to this ghost supper!

MUMMY. Do you know who is coming?

OLD MAN. Not entirely.

MUMMY. The Baron . . . who lives upstairs, and whose father-in-law was buried at noon . . .

OLD MAN. Him—who is getting a divorce in order to marry the janitor's daughter . . . Him, who was once your—lover!

MUMMY. And also your former fiancée is coming, whom my husband seduced . . .

OLD MAN. A pretty gathering . . .

MUMMY. Oh God, why can't we die? *Why* can't we die!

OLD MAN. Why do you continue to do this?

MUMMY. Our crimes, our secrets, and our guilt bind us together! — We have tried to go our separate ways many times. But we're always drawn back together again . . .

OLD MAN. I think the Colonel is coming . . .

MUMMY. Then I'll go in to Adèle . . .

(Pause)

Jacob, think of what you are doing! Spare him . . .

(Pause; she leaves)

COLONEL. *(Enters, cold and reserved.)* Be so good as to sit!

OLD MAN. *(Slowly seats himself.)*

(Pause)

COLONEL. *(Stares at him fixedly.)* Are you the one who wrote me this letter?

OLD MAN. Yes.

COLONEL. Your name is Hummel?

OLD MAN. Yes.

(Pause)

COLONEL. I know that you have bought up all of my outstanding bills; it follows therefore that you hold my whole life in your hands. What do you want of me?

OLD MAN. I will have payment, but of another sort.

COLONEL. Of what sort?

OLD MAN. A simple matter—let's not talk of money—tolerate my presence in your house, as a guest!

COLONEL. If it is a help for such a little . . .

OLD MAN. Thank you!

COLONEL. Nothing else?

OLD MAN. Dismiss Bengtsson!

COLONEL. Why should I do that? My trusted employee, who has been with me a lifetime—who earned the national medal for loyal services. — Why should I do that?

OLD MAN. That's all very nice, what you think of him — But he is not what he seems to be!

COLONEL. After all who is?

OLD MAN. *(Recoils.)* True! But Bengtsson must go!

COLONEL. Are you going to give orders in my house?

OLD MAN. Yes! After all I own everything here—furniture, curtains, dishes, linen . . . and more!

COLONEL. What do you mean more?

OLD MAN. Everything! Everything you see, it is mine!

COLONEL. Very well, it is yours! But my noble rank and good name remain mine.

OLD MAN. No, not even that.

(Pause)

You are not a nobleman.

COLONEL. How dare you!

OLD MAN. *(Takes out a piece of paper.)* If you read this extract from the national registry of titles, you will not see your name there. It died out over one hundred years ago.

COLONEL. *(Reads.)* I've heard rumors of this sort of thing. But I inherited this title from my father . . . *(reads.)* It is true; it is true . . . I am not a nobleman! — Not even that! — I can no longer wear this signet ring—but I forgot, it belongs to . . . Be so good!

OLD MAN. *(Thrusting on the ring)* Now let us continue! — You are not a colonel either!

COLONEL. I am not?

OLD MAN. No! You were commissioned a colonel in the American volunteers because of your name; but at the end of the war in Cuba and reorganization of the army, all such commissions were canceled . . .

COLONEL. Is that true?

OLD MAN. *(Reaching into his pocket)* Do you want to read about it?

COLONEL. No, it won't be necessary! . . . Who are you? What gives you the right to sit there and strip me naked like this?

OLD MAN. You shall see! But as far as stripping is concerned . . . do you know who you are?

COLONEL. You dare that much?

OLD MAN. Take off that wig of yours and look in the glass. Then take out those false teeth and shave off your mustache; let Bengtsson unlace your iron corset, so we can see if a certain servant, Mr. X, can see himself; he was the cook's lover in order to scrounge food . . .

COLONEL. *(Reaches for the bell on the table.)*

OLD MAN. *(Stops him.)* Don't touch the bell. Don't call Bengtsson; if you do, I'll order him arrested . . . here come your guests—let us be calm, so we can go on playing our old roles for a while!

COLONEL. Who are you? I seem to know your eyes and the sound of your voice . . .

OLD MAN. Don't ask, only be silent and obey!

*

STUDENT. *(Enters and bows to the* COLONEL.*)* Colonel, sir!

COLONEL. Welcome to my house, young man! Your noble conduct has brought your name to everybody's lips. And I reckon it a great honor to receive you in my home . . .

STUDENT. Colonel, sir. My poor background . . . and your famous name and your noble family . . .

COLONEL. May I present Mr. Arkenholz, Director Hummel . . . The ladies are in there, Mr. Arkenholz—if you care to join them. I have a few more things I want to say to the director . . .

STUDENT. *(Shown into the hyacinth room where he remains visible to the audience, standing in shy conversation with the* YOUNG LADY.*)*

COLONEL. A superb young man: musician, singer, writer, poet . . . if only he were a nobleman and equal to me, I certainly would have nothing against my . . . hmmm . . .

OLD MAN. My what?

COLONEL. My daughter . . .

OLD MAN. *Your* daughter!—Apropos of her, why does she always sit in that room?

COLONEL. She feels compelled to sit in the hyacinth room when she's in the house. It's a quirk of hers . . . Here comes Miss Beatrice von Holsteinkrona . . . A charming woman . . . A pillar of the church and with a fine income for her position and circumstances . . .

OLD MAN. *(To himself)* My fiancée.

*

FIANCÉE. *(Enters, she appears to be crazy.)*

COLONEL. Miss Holsteinkrona, Director Hummel . . .

FIANCÉE. *(Curtsies and sits.)*

*

ARISTOCRAT. *(Enters in a mysterious manner, dressed in mourning, and sits.)*

COLONEL. Baron Skanskorg . . .

OLD MAN. *(Aside, without rising)* I'd think him a jewel thief . . . *(To the* COLONEL*)* Let out the mummy, so the party can begin . . .

COLONEL. *(In the doorway to the hyacinth room)* Polly!

*

MUMMY. *(Enters.)* Kurrrrr-e!

COLONEL. Shall we have the young people in also?

OLD MAN. No! Not youth! They shall be spared . . . *(Now everyone sits in a silent circle.)*

COLONEL. Shall we have tea?

OLD MAN. Why bother? No one cares for tea and therefore why should we sit and pretend.

(Pause)

COLONEL. Shall we converse then?

OLD MAN. *(Slowly and with pauses)* Talk of the weather, which we know; ask how we are, that we know. I prefer silence, to hear men thinking and see their pasts; silence can hide nothing . . . But words can; I read recently that different languages arose so that primitive man might keep his tribal secrets from the others. Spoken words are ciphers and if one can find the key then one can understand all tongues of the world; but one can also uncover secrets without a key, and especially in the matter of one's parentage; when it is necessary for legal proof that is another matter: two false witnesses are all the legal proof needed, if they agree. But for the venture I have in mind I have no need of witnesses. Nature herself has endowed human beings with a sense of shame that seeks to bury what should be buried. Nevertheless we find ourselves in situations against our will when by chance our deepest secrets must be uncovered, when the mask is torn from the impostor, when the criminal is exposed . . .

(Pause; all regard each other silently.)

How hushed you are!

(Long silence)

Here, for example, in this respectable house, in their lovely home, where beauty, culture, and wealth unite . . .

(Long silence)

All we who sit here, we know who we are . . . don't we? . . .
I don't need to say that . . . and you recognize me, though
you pretend not to . . . In that other room sits my daughter,
mine; you know that also . . . She has lost the desire to live,
without knowing why . . . but she is withering in this air so
fouled with crime, treachery, and all kinds of falsehood . . .
For this reason I sought her a friend whose very nearness
will cause her to discover the light and warmth of noble
deeds . . .

    (Long silence)

This has been my mission in this house: to root out weeds,
to expose crimes, to balance the ledger, so that youth may
start anew in their home, which I present to them!

    (Long silence)

Now I grant you freedom to leave, each of you in turn; him
who stays I'll have arrested!

    (Long silence)

Do you hear the clock ticking, the death clock on the wall!
Do you hear what she is saying? "Time goes! Time goes! —
— —"

When she strikes, in a little while, then your time is run out,
then you may go but not before. She raises her arms first
before she strikes!—Listen! She warns you: "The clock can
strike."— — — I also can strike . . . *(He strikes the table with
his crutch.)*

Do you hear?

    (Silence)

    MUMMY. *(Goes over to the pendulum and stops it; then speaking
clearly and seriously.)* But I can stop time in its course—I can
wipe away the past, undo what's done; not with bribes, not
with threats—but through suffering and repentance— — —
(Goes over to the OLD MAN.*)* We are pitiable mortals, that we
know; we have erred, we have sinned, we, like all; we are not
what we seem to be, but we have a better self hidden within
us, for we regret our failings. But that you Jacob Hummel
with your false name should dare sit in judgment proves
you are worse than we poor sinners! You are no more what
you seem to be than we are! — You are a thief of men's
souls, for you have stolen mine with false promises; you have
murdered the Consul who was buried today, you strangled
him with bills; you have stolen the student also and bind him

with an imaginary debt of his father who never owed you a penny . . .

OLD MAN. *(Has attempted to raise himself and say something, but he has fallen back into a chair and has crumpled, crumpling more and more during the following.)*

MUMMY. All this shows a dark blot in your life, which I don't rightly know, merely guessing . . . I believe Bengtsson has the facts on that!

(Rings the table bell.)

OLD MAN. No, not Bengtsson! Not him!

MUMMY. Aha. *He* knows it! *(Ringing again)*

(Now the little MILKMAID *appears in the hallway, unseen by anyone with the exception of the* OLD MAN, *who is terrified; the* MILKMAID *vanishes when* BENGTSSON *enters.)*

Do you, Bengtsson, know this man?

BENGTSSON. Yes, I know him and he, me. Life reverses things we know, and I serve in his house as he has once served in mine. He was a lover to the cook in my kitchen for two whole years. — Because he had to leave at three o'clock she gave him his meal at two o'clock and the household made do with warmed-over meat that he left—then too he drank all the meat's juices so we had soup made only of water. — He sat there like a vampire and sucked all the marrow out of our house so that we became like skeletons and he had all of us put in prison when we accused the cook of thieving.

Later I met this same man in Hamburg using an assumed name. He'd now become a loan shark, another sort of bloodsucker. But then charges were brought against him for luring a girl out on the ice in order to drown her, because he feared she'd witnessed a crime he did not want to be exposed . . .

MUMMY. *(Passing her hand over the* OLD MAN*'s face)* This is you! Now bring forth the bills and the Will!

JOHANSSON. *(Appears in the hall doorway and watches the scene with great interest, for he knows this will release him from his slavery.)*

OLD MAN. *(Takes out a bundle of papers and throws them on the table.)*

MUMMY. *(Stroking the* OLD MAN*'s back)* Parrot! Is Jacob there?

OLD MAN. *(Like a parrot)* Jacob is there!—Cock-a-doodle-do-oo!

MUMMY. Can the clock strike?

OLD MAN. *(Clucking)* The clock can strike. *(Imitates a cuckoo clock.)* Cuc-koo, Cuc-koo, Cuc-koo! . . .

MUMMY. *(Opening the clothes-closet door)* Now the clock has struck! — Get up, go into the clothes closet where I sat for twenty years and mourned our crime. — In there hangs a rope which can remind you of the rope with which you strangled the Consul, and with which you planned to strangle your benefactor . . . Go!

OLD MAN. *(Goes into the clothes closet.)*

MUMMY. *(Closes the door.)* Bengtsson! Set the screen out! Death's screen!

BENGTSSON. *(Sets the screen in front of the door.)*

MUMMY. It is finished!—God have pity on his soul!

EVERYONE. Amen!

(Long silence)

*

(In the hyacinth room, the YOUNG LADY *appears with a harp on which she accompanies the* STUDENT*'s recitation.)*

SONG: *(with a short prelude)*

> I gazed into the sun
>> Until I seemed to see
> The ever-hidden One
>> Behind Infinity.
> And, beaming forth, the sun
>> This lyric sang to me:
> All men exist through pain-
>> ful work, as you can see.
>
> Yet this alone his gain,
>> His immortality,
> And blessed is the one
>> Who helps his enemy.
> The seeds that anger sows
>> Return but ill, you see;
> The greatest work man knows
>> Is love and charity.

(It is a room in somewhat bizarre style, oriental motif. Hyacinths in all colors everywhere. On the tiled stove sits a great Buddha with a bulb in his lap and from this the stem of an Ascalon flower shoots up, bearing its globular cluster of white star-flowers.

Upstage right, a door to the round salon: There one can see the COLONEL *and the* MUMMY *sitting silent and motionless; part of the death screen is in sight. Left: the door to serving room and kitchen.*

The STUDENT *and the* YOUNG LADY *(Adèle) are at the table; she with a harp; he standing.)*

YOUNG LADY. Sing now for my flowers.

STUDENT. Is this your soul's blossoming.

YOUNG LADY. It is mine alone! Don't you love hyacinths?

STUDENT. I love them over all others, its virginlike form so straight and slender raises itself from the bulb, floating on water and sinking its white, pure roots into the colorless fluid; I love its colors: the snow-white, innocent, pure; the honey-gold, sweet; the pink, youthful; the red, ripe; but over all others the blue, dewey blue, the deep-eyed, the steadfast . . . I loved them since I was a child, have worshipped them, because they signify all the fine things I want . . . And yet! . . .

YOUNG LADY. What?

STUDENT. My love is unrequited, for these lovely blossoms hate me . . .

YOUNG LADY. How?

STUDENT. Their scent, strong and pure as spring's first winds which have blown forth over melting snows, confuse my senses, deafen me, blind me, thrust me out of the room, pierce me with venomous arrows that make my heart ache and my head burn! Do you not know this flower's legend?

YOUNG LADY. Tell it!

STUDENT. First its meaning. The bulb is the earth which floats on water or lies in soil; then the stem shoots up, straight as the world's axis, and there over all rest the six-pointed star flowers.

YOUNG LADY. Above the world—stars! Oh, that is grand, how did you learn that, where did you see it?

STUDENT. Let me think — In your eyes! — It is therefore an image of the Cosmos . . . For this reason, Buddha sits with the bulb of the world, watching with his unblinking eyes as it spreads out and up transforming itself into a heaven. This wretched world shall become a heaven! For this, Buddha waits!

YOUNG LADY. Now I see—Is not a snowflake also six-pointed like the hyacinth lily?

STUDENT. You are right! — Snowflakes are falling stars . . .

YOUNG LADY. And the snowdrop is a snow star . . . grown out of snow.

STUDENT. But Sirius, the largest and most beautiful of the stars in the firmament is red and gold, that is the narcissus with its gold and red cup and six white petals . . .

YOUNG LADY. Have you seen the Ascalon in bloom?

STUDENT. Yes, indeed I have! — It bears its blooms in a ball, a globe resembling the heavenly sphere studded with white stars . . .

YOUNG LADY. Yes, God, how wonderful! Whose conception was that?

STUDENT. Yours!

YOUNG LADY. Yours!

STUDENT. Ours! — We have given birth to it together, we are wedded . . .

YOUNG LADY. Not yet . . .

STUDENT. What remains?

YOUNG LADY. Waiting, Trials, Suffering!

STUDENT. Very well! Try me! *(Pause)* Tell me! Why do your parents sit in there so silently, without saying a single word?

YOUNG LADY. Because they have nothing to say to each other, because neither believes what the other says. My father has put it thus: What will it serve to speak, we can neither fool the other?

STUDENT. That is horrible to hear . . .

YOUNG LADY. Here comes the cook . . . Look at her, so big and fat she is . . .

STUDENT. What does she want?

YOUNG LADY. She will question me about dinner, I am in charge of the household during my mother's illness . . .

STUDENT. Must we care about cooking?

YOUNG LADY. We have to eat . . . Look at the cook, I cannot look at her . . .

STUDENT. Who is this ogress?

YOUNG LADY. She is of the Vampire family—Hummel; she is eating us up . . .

STUDENT. Why don't you dismiss her?

YOUNG LADY. She won't go! We have no power over her, we got her because of our sins . . . Can't you see we are wasting away, pining . . .

STUDENT. Aren't you given any meat?

YOUNG LADY. Yes, we get many dishes, but all the strength is gone . . . She boils our meat, gives us sinews and water, while she herself drinks the bouillon; and if there is roast she boils out the marrow first, eats the gravy, drinks the blood; all that she touches loses its juices, it is as though she can suck with her eyes; we get the grounds when she has drunk the coffee, she drains our wine bottles and they are filled with water . . .

STUDENT. Get rid of her!

YOUNG LADY. We cannot!

STUDENT. Why not?

YOUNG LADY. We don't know! She won't go! No one has power over her. — She has drained the strength from us!

STUDENT. Can I rid you of her!

YOUNG LADY. No! It is as it shall be! — Now that she is here! She will question me what I will have for dinner, I answer this and that; she has objections and so it happens that she does what she wills.

STUDENT. Let her decide for herself then!

YOUNG LADY. That she will not do.

STUDENT. This is a strange house. It is bewitched!

YOUNG LADY. Yes! — But now she is turning away, because she sees you!

*

COOK. *(In doorway)* No, that was not the reason!
(She grins so that she shows her teeth.)

STUDENT. Out, creature!

COOK. If I please! *(Pause)* Now I please!
(Vanishes.)

YOUNG LADY. Don't let it anger you! — Train yourself through suffering; she is only one of the trials we are undergoing in our home! For we have a housemaid also! Her we have to clean up after!

STUDENT. Now I'm sinking! *Cor in Aethere!* Sing!

YOUNG LADY. Wait!

STUDENT. Sing!

YOUNG LADY. Suffering! — This room is called the room of trials — It is beautiful to look upon, but in actuality everything is flawed . . .

STUDENT. Incredible; but such things one can overlook! Beautiful it is, but a little cold. Why isn't the fire lit?

YOUNG LADY. Because the smoke comes in.

STUDENT. Can't one remove the soot?

YOUNG LADY. That does not help! . . . Do you see that writing desk?

STUDENT. Unusually beautiful!

YOUNG LADY. But it wobbles. Every day I place a piece of cork under that leg, but the housemaid takes it out when she sweeps and I have to cut a new one. Every morning the penholder is smudged black and also the inkstand; I have to wash them up after her, every day as sure as the sun rises. *(Pause)* Think of the worst chore you know?

STUDENT. Sorting dirty laundry! Hu!

YOUNG LADY. That is mine to do! Hu!

STUDENT. And more?

YOUNG LADY. To be awakened from my sleep at night, because I have to get up and see to a rattling window . . . which the maid left open.

STUDENT. And more?

YOUNG LADY. To climb up on a ladder and fix the damper cord after the maid has yanked it down.

STUDENT. And more?

YOUNG LADY. To sweep after her, to dust after her, and to light the fire in the stove after her, she only puts in the wood! To set the damper, to wipe the glasses, to set the table *over again,* uncork the bottles, open the windows, and air out, make my bed *over again,* scald the water carafe when it has become green with slime, shop for matches and soap, which are always scarce, wipe the lamp chimneys and trim the wicks so that the lamps will not smoke; and so that they do not go out when we have company I have to fill them myself . . .

STUDENT. Sing!

YOUNG LADY. Wait! — First labor, the labor that holds life's grime away from us.

STUDENT. But you are wealthy, have two servants!

YOUNG LADY. That doesn't help! Even if we had three! It is a burden to live, and I am growing weary . . . Think if there were a nursery as well!

STUDENT. The greatest of joys . . .

YOUNG LADY. The costliest . . . Is life worth so great a burden?

STUDENT. That depends on the return one wants for his labors . . . I would shrink from nothing to win your hand.

YOUNG LADY. Don't talk so! — You can never have me!

STUDENT. Why not?

YOUNG LADY. That you must never ask.

(Pause)

STUDENT. You dropped your bracelet out of the window . . .

YOUNG LADY. Because my hand has grown so thin . . .

(Pause)

COOK. *(Appears with a Japanese flask in hand.)*

YOUNG LADY. It is she eating at me, and all of us.

STUDENT. What is in her hand?

YOUNG LADY. It's a bottle of coloring with scorpion letters on it! It is soya, which turns water into bouillon, to pass for gravy; which one adds to boiled cabbage in order to serve it as turtle soup.

STUDENT. Out!

COOK. You suck the marrow from us, and we from you; we take blood and give water back—with coloring. This is dye! — Now I go, but I stay all the same, as long as I will it! *(Goes.)*

STUDENT. Why does Bengtsson wear a medal?

YOUNG LADY. To show his great merits.

STUDENT. Has he no flaws?

YOUNG LADY. Yes, many great ones, but for them one does not have medals.

(They laugh.)

STUDENT. You have many secrets here in this house . . .

YOUNG LADY. Like all others . . . Allow us to keep ours!

(Pause)

STUDENT. Do you love honesty?

YOUNG LADY. Yes, with moderation!

STUDENT. There comes over me at times a raging desire to say everything I'm thinking; but I know the world would stop altogether if men were entirely honest. *(Pause)* I went to a funeral the other day ... In church — It was most impressive and beautiful!

YOUNG LADY. It was Director Hummel's?

STUDENT. My false benefactor, yes! — At the coffin's head stood an older friend of the deceased, and he held the funeral mace; the priest made a deep impression on me with his dignified manner and his touching words. — I wept; we all wept. — Afterwards we went to a tavern ... There I learned that the man who had held the mace loved the son of the deceased ...

YOUNG LADY. *(Stares, trying to determine the meaning.)*

STUDENT. And that the deceased borrowed money of his son's admirer ... *(Pause)* The very next day the priest was caught pocketing donations to his church! — That is beautiful!

YOUNG LADY. Whew!

(Pause)

STUDENT. Would you like to know what I think of you now?

YOUNG LADY. Don't say it, or I'll die!

STUDENT. I must, otherwise I'll die! ...

YOUNG LADY. In asylums men say everything they're thinking ...

STUDENT. Absolutely so! — My father ended up in a madhouse ...

YOUNG LADY. Was he sick?

STUDENT. No, he was healthy, but he was a lunatic! Then, it suddenly was brought out, and under the following conditions ... He had like all of us a circle of acquaintances whom he for brevity's sake called friends; they were a shallow crowd like most common men. But he felt he had to associate with them, after all he couldn't stand being alone. Well now, men don't say what they think of each other, in everyday life, and he didn't either. He knew very well how false they were, he had traced their faithlessness to the bottom ... but he was a wise man and well brought up, and so he was always polite. But one day he held a grand party—it was in the evening; he was tired from the day's work, and from always holding his tongue, while chattering filth with his guests . . .

YOUNG LADY. *(Terrified)*

STUDENT. Well now, at the table he rapped for silence, raised his glass and began to speak . . . Then the safety catch gave way, and in a long discourse he stripped the whole party naked, and after that showed them each their false-hood. And then, tired, he sat down on the middle of the table and told them all to go to hell!

YOUNG LADY. Whew!

STUDENT. I was nearby, and I will always see what happened then! . . . Father and mother exchanged blows; guests rushed for the doors . . . and father was taken to the mad-house where he died! *(Pause)* Holding one's tongue is like still-standing water which rots, and so is it in this house also. There is something rotting here! And I thought this was paradise, when I first saw you enter here . . . There I stood on a Sunday morning outside looking in; I saw a colonel who was not a colonel, I had an elderly benefactor who turned out to be a crook and had to hang himself; I saw a mummy who wasn't that at all and an old maid, but where is her virginity to be found? Where is beauty found? In nature and in my own mind where it is always in Sunday clothes! Where are honor and faithfulness found? In legends and children's tales! Where is anything that fulfills its promise? . . . In my fantasy! — Now your flowers have poisoned me and I am giving your gift back. — I asked you to marry me and share my home, we sang and played, it was poetry, and then the cook intruded . . . *Sursum Corda!* Try once more to strike the purple fire from your golden harp . . . Try, I beg you, on bended knee . . . Well, then I shall do it myself! *(Takes up the harp, but the strings do not sound.)* It is dumb and deaf! To think that the most lovely blossoms can be so poisonous, can be the most poisonous; it is a curse that hangs over the whole of creation and life . . . Why were you not willing to be my bride? Because the very core of your life is sickness. Now I can feel the Vampire in the kitchen beginning to suck on me; I believe she is a Lamia who lives on children. It is always in the kitchen where a family's children are nipped in the bud, if it hasn't already happened in the bedroom . . . One finds poisons that blind, and poisons that open eyes—I must have been born full of the latter, for I cannot see the ugly as beautiful, nor can I call evil good, I cannot! Jesus Christ descended to hell, that was his pilgrimage to earth, this madhouse, pest-house, whorehouse earth; and madmen killed him when he wished to free them, but the thief was let loose, criminals always get sympathy! — Woe! Woe unto us all. Savior of the world, save us; we perish!

(The YOUNG LADY *has shrunk together like one dying; she rings;* BENGTSSON *enters.)*

YOUNG LADY. Come with the screen! Quick — I'm dying!
*(*BENGTSSON *returns with the screen, which he opens out and places before the* YOUNG LADY.*)*

STUDENT. The Deliverer cometh! Welcome, Dear One, pale and gentle!—Sleep Thou lovely, unhappy, innocent one, suffering through no taint of your own; sleep without dreaming, and when thou awakenest . . . may a sun which cannot burn greet thee, in a home without dust, among friends beyond reproach, to a perfect love . . . Thou wise, gentle Buddha, who sits waiting for a heaven to sprout from this earth, grant us patience in our time of trial, purify our will, that thy hopes may come to pass!

(There is a humming in the strings of the harp; the room is filled with a white light.)

> I gaze into the sun
>   And surely now I see
> The ever-hidden One
>   Behind Infinity.
> And, beaming forth, the sun
>   This lyric sang to me:
> All men exist through pain-
>   ful work, as you can see.
>
> Yet this alone his gain,
>   His immortality,
> And blessed is the one
>   Who helps his enemy.
> The seeds that anger sows
>   Return but ill, you see;
> The greatest work man knows
>   Is love and charity.

(A moaning sound is heard from behind the screen.)
You poor little child, child of this world of delusion, guilt, suffering, and death; this forever changing, ever disappointing, and painful world! God in Heaven grant you mercy on your journey . . .

(The room vanishes; Boecklin's painting "Isle of the Dead" appears; soft music, tranquil, emanating sorrow, is heard coming forth from it.)

quite young, with a lively expression and cheerful, piercing eyes, yet with a suggestion of weariness. She is dressed in elegant traveling clothes.)

MRS. MAIA. *(Sits for a while as though expecting the* PROFESSOR *to say something. Then lets her newspaper fall and sighs)* Oh, no, no—!

PROFESSOR RUBEK. *(Looking up from his paper)* Well, Maia? What is wrong with you?

MAIA. Listen to the silence here.

RUBEK. *(Smiling tolerantly)* And you can hear that?

MAIA. What?

RUBEK. This silence?

MAIA. Yes, I can, really.

RUBEK. Well, you could be right, My Child. It is possible for one to perceive the condition of silence.

MAIA. Yes, God knows you can. When it is as overpowering as it is here—

RUBEK. Here at the Baths, you mean?

MAIA. I mean everywhere here at home. In the city there was noise and uproar enough. But nevertheless—I sensed that this same noise and uproar had something dead shrouding it.

RUBEK. *(With an inquiring glance)* Are you not completely happy that you have come home again, Maia?

MAIA. *(Looking at him)* Are *you* happy?

RUBEK. *(Unrevealingly)* I—?

MAIA. Yes. You have been away so much, much longer than I. Are *you* really happy now that you are home again?

RUBEK. No—in truth—Not so very happy—

MAIA. *(Animatedly)* Finally you see that! I was certain of *that* all along!

RUBEK. Perhaps I have been away too long. I'm above all this now—this provincial life here.

MAIA. *(Eagerly, pulling her chair near to him)* Now you see that, Rubek! Then we must travel on our way again. As quickly as we can.

RUBEK. *(A bit impatiently)* Yes—Yes, that is our intention, dearest Maia. You know that.

MAIA. Then why not now at once? Remember how lazy and comfortable we have it down there in our darling new house—

RUBEK. *(Smiling tolerantly)* By rights we should say: Our darling new *home.*

MAIA. *(Curtly)* I prefer to say *house.* Leave it at that.

RUBEK. *(His gaze dwelling on her)* You are, underneath it all, an odd little person.

MAIA. Am I so odd?

RUBEK. Yes, I sense that.

MAIA. But why? Perhaps because I am not inclined to lying about and adapting to the surroundings up here—?

RUBEK. Which of us demanded, dead or alive, that we travel north this summer?

MAIA. Well, that was me.

RUBEK. Yes, it certainly was not I.

MAIA. But dear God—Who could have known that everything would have been so appallingly transformed here at home! And in so short a time! I know good and well it is no more than four years since I went abroad—

RUBEK. —since you married, yes.

MAIA. Married? What has *that* to do with the matter?

RUBEK. *(Continuing)* —became the Professor's Wife and got yourself a magnificent home—pardon me—a palatial house, I should say. And a villa on Lake Taunitz, just where it is most fashionable right now—. Yes, Maia, it is both elegant and comfortable, you cannot deny that, and spacious also. We needn't always be hanging about in each other's way.

MAIA. *(Offhandedly)* No, no, no—rooms and things of that sort, there was no lack of that—

RUBEK. Also you moved in finer and more elevated surroundings. In more gracious society than here at home.

MAIA. *(Looking at him)* Well, you think it is *me* who has changed?

RUBEK. Yes, I think I mean that, Maia.

MAIA. Only me? Not people here?

RUBEK. Oh yes, they also. A bit perhaps. And not at all in a way that is lovable. I concede that.

MAIA. Yes, you certainly must concede that.

RUBEK. *(Going on)* Do you know what feelings come over me when I see the lives of the people around me here?

MAIA. No? What?

RUBEK. There comes over me a memory of the night we traveled up here by train—

MAIA. You just sat there asleep in your compartment.

RUBEK. Not entirely. I noted how it became so silent at all the small stopping places—. I *heard* silence,—like you, Maia—

MAIA. Hm. — Like me, yes.

RUBEK. And then I understood that we had come across the boundary. Now we were really home. And at every small stopping place the train halted—even though there was no traffic there.

MAIA. Why did it stop *so* still. When nothing was there?

RUBEK. I don't know. No one got off and no one got on. And the train held still for a long, endless wait, all the same. And at each station I could distinguish two train-men who walked the platform, — they each had a lantern in hand, — and they talked with each other muffled and soundless and meaningless in the night.

MAIA. Yes, you are right. There was always a pair of men who talked together—

RUBEK. —about nothing. *(Changing to a quicker tone)* But wait until tomorrow. The great luxury liner will dock. We'll go aboard and sail around the coast—Northward ho—right into the polar sea.

MAIA. But that way you will see nothing of the country—and of living. And that is what you said you wanted.

RUBEK. *(Curtly, indignantly)* I have seen more than enough.

MAIA. Do you believe that a sea voyage will be better for you?

RUBEK. It is always a change.

MAIA. Yes, yes, if it is good for *you,* then—

RUBEK. For me? Good? I don't feel anything in the world wrong with me.

MAIA. *(Stands up and goes over to him.)* Yes, you do, Rubek. You yourself must feel that.

RUBEK. But, dearest Maia—What could be wrong?

MAIA. *(Back of him, bending over the chair)* You tell me that. You are beginning to go about aimlessly. As if you had no place to rest—at home or abroad. You have come to dislike people lately.

RUBEK. *(A bit sarcastically)* No, really—Have *you* noticed *that?*

MAIA. No one who knows you could help but notice. And it seems sad to me that you have lost all interest in your work.

RUBEK. You noticed *that* also?

MAIA. *You,* who worked so untiringly before—late and early!

RUBEK. *(Gloomily)* Yes, *before,* yes—.

MAIA. But ever since your great masterwork was out of your hands—

RUBEK. *(Nodding thoughtfully)* "Resurrection Day"—

MAIA. —which is known around the world, which has made you so famous—

RUBEK. Perhaps that is the misfortune, Maia.

MAIA. Why?

RUBEK. When I had finished my masterpiece— *(Strikes a heroic gesture with his hand.)* —for "Resurrection Day" *is* a masterpiece! Or *was* one in the beginning. No, it *is* one now. *Must, must, must* be a masterpiece!

MAIA. *(Looking at him in surprise)* Yes, Rubek—the whole world knows that.

RUBEK. *(Curtly rebuffing)* The whole world knows nothing! Understands nothing!

MAIA. Well, at least it recognizes something—

RUBEK. Something that isn't there at all, yes. Something that wasn't even in my mind. They fall into ecstasies over *that. (Grumbling to himself)* No earthly good comes from working oneself out for the mob and masses—for "the whole world."

MAIA. Do you feel it is better—it is worthy of *you* to get by with only a portrait bust from time to time?

RUBEK. *(A slow smile)* Those are not exactly portrait busts I have lowered myself to doing, Maia.

MAIA. Yes, they are, God knows—for the last two or three years—ever since you finished the great group and got it out of the house—

RUBEK. All the same they are not really *protrait* busts, I tell you.

MAIA. What are they then?

RUBEK. Something lies covered over, something shadowy far within and far back of the busts—something private, which none of the people can see—

MAIA. So?

RUBEK. *(Conclusively)* Only *I* can see it. And that amuses me to the heart. Outwardly I give them "striking likenesses," as they say, and folks stand and gape in astonishment at them—*(lowering his voice)*—but at the very foundation they are respectable, haughty horse-mugs, and stubborn ass snouts, and lop-eared, low-browed dog skulls, and bloated swine heads—and sometimes the loose hanging, brutish neck of an ox.

MAIA. *(Indifferently)* All the dear domestic animals.

RUBEK. Only the dear domesticated animals, Maia. All the animals which mankind has transmuted in his image. And some have transmuted mankind in requital. *(Emptying his champagne glass and laughing)* And these cunning works of art are the same ones which the good aristocrats come and commission from me. And pay for in good faith—and at a good commission. Worth their weight in gold, one might say.

MAIA. *(Filling his glass)* Shame, Rubek! Enjoy your drink and be happy.

RUBEK. *(Striking himself several times on the brow and leaning back in the chair)* I am happy. Really happy. In a way. *(A short silence)* For there is pleasure in being able to feel free of all obligations. Possessing all the things one could ask for oneself. All outward things that is. —Don't you feel the same, Maia?

MAIA. Oh yes, I do. That is good enough, that too. *(Looking at him)* But can't you remember what you promised me on the day we came to an understanding about—about that difficulty—

RUBEK. *(Nodding)* —came to an understanding that we should marry. That did not come easy for you, Maia.

MAIA. *(Going on undisturbed)* —And that I should journey with you to other lands and live there for a lifetime—living the good life. —Can you remember what you promised me then.

RUBEK. *(Shaking his head)* No, I can't. No, what did I promise you?

MAIA. You said you would take me with you up on a high mountain and show me all the world's glories.

RUBEK. *(Startled)* Did I actually promise *you* that also?

MAIA. *(Looking at him)* Me also? Who else?

RUBEK. *(Indifferently)* No, no, I only meant did I promise to show you—?

MAIA. —all the world's glories. Yes, you did. And all those glories shall be mine and yours, you said.

RUBEK. That was a sort of saying I used to use once upon a time.

MAIA. Only a saying?

RUBEK. Yes, something from school days. Something I said to tempt the neighbor kids with when I wanted them to come out and play with me in the woods and mountains.

MAIA. *(Looking hard at him)* Perhaps you only wanted to have *me* out to play with also?

RUBEK. *(Passing it off as a joke)* Well, hasn't it been a fairly entertaining game, Maia?

MAIA. *(Coldly)* I didn't go with you only as a game.

RUBEK. No, no, that is a fact.

MAIA. And you never did take me with you up on a high mountain and show me—

RUBEK. *(Irritated)* —all the world's glories? No, I did not. But I shall tell you something! You are not properly made to be a mountain climber, little Maia.

MAIA. *(Seeking to control herself)* Yet you seemed to feel that was so at one time.

RUBEK. Four or five years ago, yes. *(Stretching out in the chair)* Four, five years—That is a long, long time, Maia.

MAIA. *(Looking at him with a bitter expression)* Has the time seemed so very long for you, Rubek?

RUBEK. It is beginning to seem to be a bit long to me now. *(Yawning)* Once in a while.

MAIA. *(Going back to her place)* I shall not bore you longer. *(She sits in her chair, takes up her paper and leafs through it.)*

(A hush from both sides.)

RUBEK. *(Leaning on his elbows over the table and looking teasingly at her)* Is the professor's wife offended?

MAIA. *(Coldly, not looking up)* No, not in the least.

(Bath guests, mostly women, begin to come singly and in groups through the park from the right and out to the left.)

(Waiters bring refreshments from the hotel and exit behind the pavilion.)

(THE INSPECTOR, with gloves and a cane in hand, comes from his rounds in the park, meeting guests, greets them politely, and exchanges a few words with several of them.)

INSPECTOR. *(Coming forward to the* PROFESSOR *'s table and politely removing his hat)* May I offer my respects to the professor's wife. —And good morning to the Professor.

RUBEK. Good morning, good morning, Inspector.

INSPECTOR. *(Addressing himself to* MAIA *)* May one venture to inquire if you had a restful night?

MAIA. Yes, thank you; remarkably well—for *my* part. I always sleep like a stone at night.

INSPECTOR. I am pleased to hear that. The first night in a strange place can be very disagreeble. —And the Professor—?

RUBEK. Oh, I don't get much sleep at night. Especially recently.

INSPECTOR. *(A show of sympathy)* Oh—that is too bad. But after a few weeks here at the Baths—you will rid yourself of *that.*

RUBEK. *(Looking up at him)* Tell me, Inspector, —is it the custom of some of your patients to bathe at night?

INSPECTOR. *(Surprised)* At night? No I've never heard of that.

RUBEK. You haven't.

INSPECTOR. No, I know of no one *so* sick here as to require *that.*

RUBEK. Well, but is there someone whose custom it is to walk about in the park at night?

INSPECTOR. *(Smiling and shaking his head)* No, Professor, — that would be against the regulations.

MAIA. *(Becoming impatient)* Good lord, Rubek, that is what I said to you this morning, —you dreamed it.

RUBEK. *(Dryly)* So? Did I? Thanks! *(Turning to the* INSPECTOR *)* The fact is I stayed up last night; because I could not go to sleep. And since I wanted to see what kind of night it was—

INSPECTOR. *(Attentively)* Yes, Professor? Well—?

RUBEK. So I looked out of the window, —and my eye fell on a light form there in among the trees.

MAIA. *(Smiling at the* INSPECTOR *)* And the Professor claims that the form was dressed in a bathing costume.

RUBEK. —Or else something like it, I said. I could not make it out clearly. But I saw something white.

INSPECTOR. Highly remarkable. Was it a gentleman or a lady?

RUBEK. Its manner was that of a lady. But behind it there came another form. And this was very dark. Like a shadow—

INSPECTOR. *(Startled)* A dark one? Even black perhaps?

RUBEK. Yes, it appeared almost black to *my* eyes.

INSPECTOR. *(As though a light breaks in)* And following after the *white*? Following close after her—?

RUBEK. Yes. At a little distance—

INSPECTOR. Aha! Then I can give you an explanation, Professor.

RUBEK. Well, what was it?

MAIA. *(At the same time)* The professor was not asleep and dreaming!

INSPECTOR. *(Suddenly in a whisper, indicating the background to the right)* Sh-h-h, if you please! Look there—. Don't speak for just a moment!

(A slender LADY, *dressed in fine, cream-colored white cashmere and followed by a* DEACONESS *in black with a silver cross on a chain at her breast, enters from behind the hotel and crosses the park toward the pavilion in the left foreground. Her face is pale and drawn and stiffened; eyelids droop and the eyes seem to be without sight. Her dress is floor-length and form-fitting, falling in folds about her body. Over her head, neck, breasts, shoulders, and arms she has a large white crepe shawl. She holds her arms crossed over her breasts. Stands without motion. Then moves stiffly and with measured steps. The* DEACONESS'*s movements are likewise measured, and she seems like a servant. She follows the lady ceaselessly with her brown, piercing eyes. Waiters with napkins on their arms come forward in the hotel doorway and cast inquisitive glances at the two strangers, who without looking around proceed into the pavilion.)*

RUBEK. *(Has risen slowly and unwillingly from his chair and stares at the closed door of the pavilion)* Who was that lady?

INSPECTOR. A stranger who has rented the little pavilion there.

RUBEK. A foreigner?

INSPECTOR. We assume that. At any rate they came here together from abroad. A week ago now. They have never been here before.

RUBEK. *(Decisively, looking at him)* It was she I saw in the park last night.

INSPECTOR. It must have been. I thought so at once.

RUBEK. What is the lady's name, Inspector?

INSPECTOR. She has registered herself in this manner: "Madame de Satow, and companion." We know nothing more.

RUBEK. *(Thinking to himself)* Satow? Satow—?

MAIA. *(Laughing scoffingly)* Do you know someone with that name, Rubek? Eh?

RUBEK. *(Shaking his head)* No, not a one. —Satow? It sounds sort of Russian. Or Slavic at any rate. *(To the* INSPECTOR *)* What language does she speak?

INSPECTOR. When the two women talk together it is in a language which I cannot make out. But otherwise she speaks in perfect Norwegian.

RUBEK. *(Bursting out suddenly)* Norwegian! You are not mistaken in that?

INSPECTOR. No, I could not be mistaken about that.

RUBEK. *(Looking eagerly at him)* You yourself have heard her?

INSPECTOR. Yes I have talked with her. A few times — Only a few words however. For she is very reticent. But—

RUBEK. But it was Norwegian?

INSPECTOR. Clear, perfect Norwegian. Perhaps with a little touch of North country accent.

RUBEK. *(Staring straight before him and whispering)* That also.

MAIA. *(A little hurt and badly jarred)* Perhaps the lady once served as a model for you, Rubek? Do you recall?

RUBEK. *(Looking sharply at her)* Model?

MAIA. *(With a provoking smile)* Yes, in your younger years, I mean. For you are said to have had so many models. Long ago, naturally.

RUBEK. *(In the same tone)* Oh no, little Mrs. Maia. In my past I have had only one single model. One single one—for all that I have done.

INSPECTOR. *(Who has turned and is looking off to the left)* Yes, friends, but now you must excuse me. For *there* comes someone I do not care to meet up with. Especially not in a lady's presence.

RUBEK. *(Looking in the same direction)* That hunter there? Who is that?

INSPECTOR. That is Mr. Ulfheim, whose estate—

RUBEK. Oh, Mr. Ulfheim.

INSPECTOR. —Bearslayer some call him—

RUBEK. I know him.

INSPECTOR. Yes, who does not know him?

RUBEK. Only a brief introduction. Is he a patient here—finally?

INSPECTOR. No, oddly enough—not yet. He comes here only once a year, —when he is on his way up to his hunting grounds. — Pardon me a moment — *(He attempts to go into the hotel.)*

ULFHEIM. *(*ULFHEIM*'s voice, heard from outside)* Stay there a moment! Stay there, Damnation! Why are you always running away from me?

INSPECTOR. *(Stops)* I am not running away, Mr. Ulfheim. *(Estate owner* ULFHEIM *enters from the left, followed by a* SERVANT, *who guides on a leash a pair of hunting dogs.* ULFHEIM *is in shooting costume, with high boots and a felt hat with a feather in it. His is a long, meager, sinewy figure, with matted hair and beard, loud-voiced. One cannot tell his age to look at him, but he is no longer young.)*

ULFHEIM. *(Pouncing on the* INSPECTOR*)* Is *this* a way to greet strangers here, eh? You scurry off with your tail between your legs—as though you had the devil at your butt.

INSPECTOR. *(Quietly without answering him)* Did the gentleman arrive on the steamer?

ULFHEIM. *(Growling)* What steamer? *(Hands on hips)* Don't you know that I sail my own yacht? *(To the* SERVANT*)* Go care for your fellow creatures, Lars. But keep them ravenously hungry as well. Fresh meat-bones. But not much meat on them, you hear? And that should be red and dripping with blood. And get something in your own stomach also. *(Aiming a kick at him)* Now get the hell out of here.

(The SERVANT *goes out with the hounds behind the hotel.)*

INSPECTOR. Would the gentleman wish to go into the dining room a while?

ULFHEIM. In with all those half-dead flies and people? No, a thousand thanks for that, Mr. Inspector.

INSPECTOR. Yes, yes, as you please.

ULFHEIM. But have a girl get the supplies ready for me as usual. Abundant amounts of food. And lots of brandy—! You can tell her that I or Lars will come and set the Devil on her if she doesn't—

INSPECTOR. *(Interrupting)* We know you from the past. *(Turning away)* Shall I take an order for the waiter, Professor. Perhaps something for Mrs. Rubek?

RUBEK. No thank you; nothing for me.

MAIA. Nothing for me, either.

(The INSPECTOR *exits into the hotel.)*

ULFHEIM. *(Staring at them a moment, then lifts his hat)* Death and damnation. What is a peasant brat doing in this fine society?

RUBEK. *(Looking up)* I don't understand your meaning?

ULFHEIM. *(In a more polite manner)* If I am not mistaken, it is the same master artist Rubek, I would guess.

RUBEK. *(Nodding)* We have met once or twice socially the last time I was home.

ULFHEIM. Yes, that was many years ago. *Then* you were not so famous as I hear you are now. *Then* even a filthy bearslayer dared come near you.

RUBEK. *(Smiling)* I don't bite now either.

MAIA. *(Looking with interest at* ULFHEIM*)* Are *you* really and truly a bearslayer?

ULFHEIM. *(Sitting at the next table, nearer the hotel)* Bear is my preference, Madam. But otherwise I will take any sort of thing that comes my way. Eagles, or wolves, or women, or elk, or reindeer—. As long as they're fresh and juicy and full of blood, then— *(He drinks from a pocket flask.)*

MAIA. *(Looking at him fixedly)* But you prefer bear killing?

ULFHEIM. Prefer, yes. For one must always have a knife ready for them. *(Smiling a little)* We work with hard material, both of us, Madam,—both I and your husband. He toils over his marble stones, I am sure. And I toil with straining, quivering bear-muscle. And each subdues his material in the end. Till we are lord and master over it. We bend it to our will no matter how hard the struggle.

RUBEK. *(Thinking deeply)* There is much truth in what you say.

ULFHEIM. Yes, for stone also has something to struggle for, I think. It is dead and will by no means let itself be hammered to life. Exactly like the bear when one comes and prods him from his lair.

MAIA. Are you traveling up now to hunt in the woods?

ULFHEIM. Far up into the high mountains. — You have never been to the mountain heights, Madam?

MAIA. No, never.

ULFHEIM. Death and pain, then you must come up there this very summer! You can be in my company. Both you and the professor.

MAIA. Thanks. But Rubek is thinking about a sea voyage this summer.

RUBEK. The island channels along the coast.

ULFHEIM. Phew. — What the devil, it would be hellish for you in those nauseous gutters! Think a moment—lying there and wallowing in brackish water. Vomit-water, I call it.

MAIA. Do you hear that, Rubek?

ULFHEIM. No, far better to come up into the mountains with me. No sight or sign of mankind there. You cannot realize what that means to *me*. But such a little lady—*(He stops.)*

(The DEACONESS *enters from the pavilion and goes into the hotel.)*

ULFHEIM. *(Following her with his eyes)* Look there. That black bird. — Who is having a funeral?

RUBEK. I have not heard of one—

ULFHEIM. Well, someone nearby must be ready to give up the ghost. In some corner or other. — Those who are sick and poorly should have the sense to get themselves buried, — the sooner the better.

MAIA. Are you ever sick yourself, Mr. Ulfheim?

ULFHEIM. Never. Or I would not be here. — But my closest friends—sometimes they are sick.

MAIA. And what do you do for those friends?

ULFHEIM. Shoot them, naturally.

RUBEK. *(Looking at him)* Shoot them?

MAIA. *(Moving her chair back)* Shoot them dead?

ULFHEIM. *(Nodding)* My shot never misses, Madam.

MAIA. But how can you lower yourself to shoot a man dead!

ULFHEIM. I do not speak of men—

MAIA. Your friends, you said—

ULFHEIM. My closest friends, who else but my dogs.

MAIA. Your dogs are your closest friends?

ULFHEIM. I have no one nearer. My honest, faithful, trust-

RUBEK. Guilty of *that*—as you call it, your death?

IRENE. Guilty because I had to die. *(Changing to an indifferent tone)* Why don't you sit down, Arnold?

RUBEK. May I?

IRENE. Yes. — You will not be given the cold shivers. I don't think I have quite turned to ice yet.

RUBEK. *(Moves a chair and sits at her table.)* See, there, Irene. Now we two sit together as in the old days.

IRENE. A little distant from each other. Also as in the old days.

RUBEK. *(Moving nearer)* It had to be so then.

IRENE. Had to?

RUBEK.*(Continuing)* There *had* to be distance between us—

IRENE. Yes, had to be what ultimately was, Arnold?

RUBEK. *(Continuing)* Do you recall what you answered when I asked whether you would fly far away with me?

IRENE. I held up three fingers in the air and swore that I would fly with you to the world's end and to life's end. And that I would serve you in all things—

RUBEK. As a model for my works of art—

IRENE. —In free, full nakedness—

RUBEK. *(Emotionally)* And you did serve me, Irene—so bravely—so happy and reckless.

IRENE. Yes. With all my youth's throbbing blood I served you!

RUBEK. *(Nodding, with a look of thankfulness)* You have every right to say that.

IRENE. Fell down at your feet and served you, Arnold! *(Clenching her hands toward him)* But you, you — you —!

RUBEK. *(Defensively)* I never wronged you! Never, Irene!

IRENE. Yes, you did! You wronged what was born deepest in me—

RUBEK. *(Starting back)* I—!

IRENE. Yes, You! I exposed myself entirely and completely to your inspection— *(Softer)* And you never once touched me.

RUBEK. Irene, didn't you know that many a day I was beside myself because of your beauty?

IRENE. *(Continuing undisturbed)* Nevertheless—*had* you touched me, I think I would have killed you where you stood. For I had a sharp needle with me. Hidden in my hair—

(Stroking her forehead thoughtfully) Yes but—no, nevertheless
—nevertheless; — that you could—

RUBEK. *(Looking impressively at her)* I was an artist, Irene.

IRENE. *(Darkly)* Just that. Just that.

RUBEK. First and foremost an artist. And I had become
sick with determination to shape the great work of my life.
(Losing himself in remembering) It was to be called "Resurrection Day." Personified in the likeness of a young woman
awakening from the sleep of death—

IRENE. Our child, yes—

RUBEK. *(Continues.)* The world's noblest, purest, ideal
woman awakening. Then I found *you.* You were what I
needed in every way. And you agreed so happily and willingly. And you left your family and home—and joined me.

IRENE. To join with you was like a resurrection from my
childhood.

RUBEK. That very reason made you ideal. You and no
other. You became to me a sacred creation, who could only
be touched in adoring thoughts. I was still young then,
Irene. And I developed a superstition that to touch you, or
have desire for you in a sensual way, would be a profanation,
and as a consequence I should never be able to achieve what
I was striving for. — And I still believe there is some truth
in that.

IRENE. *(Nodding with a touch of scorn)* Art first—then hu-
manity.

RUBEK. Yes, you must judge me as you will. But I was
completely dedicated to my work then. And I felt jubilantly
happy in it.

IRENE. And you succeeded with your work, Arnold.

RUBEK. You have my thanks and praise for that—that I
succeeded in my work. I wished to embody a pure woman
in the way I envisioned her upon awakening on the day of
resurrection. Not in wonder over things new and unknown
and undreamed of. But full of a blessed joy on finding herself unchanged—her, the earth woman—in those higher,
freer, more joyful regions—after the long, dreamless death-
sleep. *(Speaking softer)* And that is how I shaped her. — I
shaped her in *your* image, Irene.

IRENE. *(Laying her hands flat on the table and leaning back in
her chair)* And then you were through with me—

RUBEK. *(Reproachingly)* Irene!

IRENE. —Had no further use for me—

RUBEK. How can you say *that*?

IRENE. —began to search about for another ideal—

RUBEK. I found none, none after you.

IRENE. And no other models, Arnold?

RUBEK. *You* were the only model for me. You were the source of my creativity.

IRENE. *(Silent for a little while)* Have you created any poems since? In marble, I mean. After the day I went away from you?

RUBEK. I have created no poems since that day. I have only been molding trifles.

IRENE. And that woman you are now living with—?

RUBEK. *(Interrupting fiercely)* Don't speak of her now! That strikes me to the heart.

IRENE. Where do you plan to travel with her?

RUBEK. *(Slack and tired)* A long, tedious voyage north along the coast.

IRENE. *(Looking at him, smiling almost imperceptively and whispering)* Travel instead high up among the mountains. As high up as you can go. Higher, higher—ever higher, Arnold.

RUBEK. *(Tense with expectation)* Are *you* going up there?

IRENE. Have you the spirit to join with me one more time?

RUBEK. *(Struggling, uncertain)* If only we could—Oh, if only we could—

IRENE. Why can't we do what we want to? *(Looking at him and whispering pleadingly with folded hands)* Come, come, Arnold! Oh, come up with me—

(MAIA enters blooming with happiness from behind the hotel and hastens to the table where she had been sitting.)

MAIA. *(Still near the hotel, without looking around)* Now I know what you will say, Rubek, but—*(Stops as her eye falls on* IRENE*)* Oh, excuse me—you have made an acquaintance I see.

RUBEK. *(Curtly)* Renewed an acquaintance. *(Standing up)* What is it you wanted of me?

MAIA. Just this—that *you* may do whatever you please— but *I* will not travel with you on that disgusting steamer.

RUBEK. Why not?

MAIA. No, I want to go up on the mountains and into the woods—I do. *(Coaxingly)* Oh, you must let me, Rubek!—I shall be so good, so good ever after.

RUBEK. Who has put this in your head?

MAIA. Him. That awful bearslayer. Oh, you cannot imagine all the wonders he has to tell of the mountains. And the life up there! Ugly, awful, repulsive stories and lies he spins —. Yes, I believe they are all lies. But so wonderfully alluring at the same time. Oh won't you let me go with him? Only so that I can see how much of it is true, do you understand? May I, Rubek?

RUBEK. Yes, all right. Go up into the mountains—as far and as long as you please. Perhaps I will travel the same way.

MAIA. *(Quickly)* No, no, no, you don't need to do that! Not for *my* sake!

RUBEK. I *want* to go to the mountains. I am determined about that now.

MAIA. Oh, thanks, thanks! May I tell the bearslayer at once?

RUBEK. Tell the bearslayer whatever you wish.

MAIA. Oh, thanks, thanks, thanks! *(Tries to grab his hand; he withdraws it.)* Oh, no—but you are sweet and good today, Rubek! *(She runs into the hotel.)*

(At the same time the door to the pavilion opens and stands silently ajar. The DEACONESS *stands intently on watch inside the door's opening. No one sees her.)*

RUBEK. *(Decidedly, turning to* IRENE*)* Shall we also reunite up there?

IRENE. *(Rising slowly)* Yes, we certainly shall—I have sought so long after you.

RUBEK. When did you begin to seek after me, Irene?

IRENE. *(With a tinge of sarcasm)* From the time I realized that I had given up to you something priceless, Arnold. Something one should never part with.

RUBEK. *(Bowing his head)* Yes, that's true. I'll always regret that. You gave me three or four years of your youth.

IRENE. More, more than *that* I gave you. It was wasted—what I gave you.

RUBEK. Yes, a wastrel you were, Irene. You gave me all your naked loveliness—

IRENE. —to contemplate—

RUBEK. —and to glorify—

IRENE. Yes, for your own glorification—and for the child's.

RUBEK. For you also, Irene.

IRENE. But the most precious gift you have forgotten.

RUBEK. Most precious—? Which gift was *that*?

IRENE. I gave you my young, living soul. And that left me empty within—soulless. *(Looks fixedly at him)* It was *that* I died of, Arnold.

(The DEACONESS *opens the door wide and makes room for her.)*

(She exits into the pavilion.)

RUBEK. *(Stands and looks after her; then he whispers)* Irene!

Second Act

(Near a sanatorium high in the mountains. The landscape stretches, an immense treeless upland plain, to a long mountain lake. On the other side of the lake rises a row of high peaks with bluish-white snow in the clefts. In the foreground to the left the divided streamlets of a brook run down a rock wall and thence across the plain and out to the right. Scrub brush, plants, and stones edge the brook. In the foreground to the right a rise with a stone bench on its top. It is a summer afternoon, along toward sunset.

At some distance over the vast plain on the other side of the brook a flock of singing children are playing and dancing. Some are in town-made clothes, others in peasant garb. Their laughter in the distance is heard under the following scene.

PROFESSOR RUBEK *is sitting on the bench with a plaid robe over his shoulders, looking down on the children at play.*

Shortly thereafter MAIA *enters from among some bushes on the plain to the left in the middle ground and scans the area with her hand shadowing her eyes. She wears a flat tourist hat, short hitched-up skirts reaching only midway between ankle and knee, and high, heavy laced boots. In her hand she has a long walking staff.)*

MAIA. *(At last she sees* PROFESSOR RUBEK *and calls)* Halloo! *(She comes forward on the plain, vaulting with the aid of her staff over the brook, and climbs up the hillside.)*

MAIA. *(Panting)* I have been rushing about looking for you, Rubek.

RUBEK. *(Nodding indifferently, asks)* Have you come from the sanatorium?

MAIA. Yes, I have just come from that fly trap.

RUBEK. *(Looking at her a moment)* You were not at the dinner table, I noticed.

MAIA. No, we had our dinner under the open skies, we two.

RUBEK. "We two"? To whom do you refer?

MAIA. I—and that awful bearslayer, of course.

RUBEK. Is that the case?

MAIA. Yes. And early tomorrow we go forth again.

RUBEK. After bear?

MAIA. Off to slay Bruin.

RUBEK. Have you found the spoor of one?

MAIA. *(Superior tone)* One does not find bear up here on the naked mountains, you know.

RUBEK. Where, then?

MAIA. Deep down. Down the trail, in the deepest woods. Where it is unpassable for common townsmen—

RUBEK. And you two plan to go there tomorrow?

MAIA. *(Casting herself down in the heather)* Yes, we have arranged that — Or perhaps we shall set off this evening. — If you have nothing against it?

RUBEK. I? No, far be it from me—

MAIA. *(Hastily)* Lars will go with us; naturally—with the dogs.

RUBEK. I have hardly been inquiring about Mr. Lars and his dogs. *(Changing subject)* Wouldn't you rather sit properly here on the bench?

MAIA. *(Drowsily)* No, thanks. I'm comfortable here in the soft heather.

RUBEK. I can see that you are tired.

MAIA. *(Yawning)* I think I am beginning to be.

RUBEK. That always follows. When the tension is over—

MAIA. *(In a sleepy tone)* Yes. I'll just close my eyes for a moment.

(Short Pause)

MAIA. *(Suddenly impatient)* Ugh, Rubek—How can you bear to sit and listen to those screaming children! And watch all the horsing around they do.

RUBEK. There is something harmonious—almost like music—in their movements occasionally. Amid all that awkwardness. And in a singular way it amuses me to watch for those moments—when they happen.

MAIA. *(Laughing a bit scornfully)* Yes, you are always the artist, you are.

RUBEK. And I am determined to remain just that.

MAIA. *(Rolling on her side so that she turns her back on him)* There's not a trace of the artist about him.

RUBEK. *(Attentively)* Nothing of the artist? Who?

MAIA. *(Again in a sleepy tone)* Him, the other, well.

RUBEK. The bear shooter, you mean?

MAIA. Yes. No trace of the artist about him. No trace.

RUBEK. *(Smiling)* No, there can be no doubt of that.

MAIA. *(Vehemently, without moving)* And how ugly he is! *(Pulls up a tuft of heather and casts it away.)* So ugly, so ugly! Ish!

RUBEK. Is that what makes you so confident to set out with him—out into the wild places?

MAIA. *(Curtly)* I don't know. *(Turns toward him)* You are also ugly, Rubek.

RUBEK. You have just discovered that?

MAIA. No, I saw it long ago.

RUBEK. *(Shrugging his shoulders)* One ages. One ages, Mrs. Maia.

MAIA. That is not what I mean. A tired, resigned look has come into your eyes — When you dare cast them on me — now and then.

RUBEK. You've seen that?

MAIA. *(Nodding)* Little by little this evil look has come into your eyes. Almost as though you are plotting a dark scheme against me.

RUBEK. Indeed? *(Friendly, but earnestly)* Come here and sit beside me, Maia. We must have a little talk.

MAIA. *(Half sitting)* May I sit on your knee? Like those first years?

RUBEK. No, you may not. Folks can see us here from the hotel. *(Moving a little)* But you can sit here on the bench beside me.

MAIA. No, thanks; I'd rather lie where I am. I can hear well enough from here. *(Looks inquiringly at him.)* Well, what is this thing we must talk about?

RUBEK. *(Beginning slowly)* What do you think was the reason I agreed for us to take this summer's trip?

MAIA. Well—I remember you said that I would get a lot of good out of it. But—

RUBEK. But—?

MAIA. But now I no longer have the least belief in that—

RUBEK. And what do you think now?

MAIA. I think now it was for that pale woman's sake.

RUBEK. Madame Von Satow—!

MAIA. Yes, she who hangs at our heels. Last night she appeared up here also.

RUBEK. But what in all the world—!

MAIA. Oh, you were acquainted with her all right—intimately so! Long before you met *me*.

RUBEK. I had forgotten her also—long before I met you.

MAIA. *(Sitting upright)* Can you forget so easily, Rubek?

RUBEK. *(Curtly)* Yes, very easily. *(Adding harshly)* When I want to forget.

MAIA. Even a woman who has been your model?

RUBEK. *(Dismissing it)* When I have no more use for her, then—

MAIA. One who has stripped herself before you?

RUBEK. That means nothing. Not to us artists. *(Striking out in a new tone)* Also, how—I ask you—how was *I* to know she would be here in this part of the country?

MAIA. Oh, you could have read her name on a guest list. In one of your papers.

RUBEK. Yes, but I had no idea of the name she now goes by, had never heard of this Herr Von Satow.

MAIA. *(Pretending to be tired)* Well, Good Lord, then there must have been some other reason behind your determination to take this journey.

RUBEK. *(Seriously)* Yes, Maia—there *was* something behind it. Something entirely different. And it is *that* reason which we must discuss here and now.

MAIA. *(Suppressing her laughter)* Jesus, what a solemn statement.

RUBEK. *(Studying her with mistrust)* Yes, perhaps a bit more solemn than necessary.

MAIA. Necessary—?

RUBEK. But *that* will have to do for both of us.

MAIA. You begin to make me curious, Rubek.

RUBEK. Only curious? Not a little uneasy?

MAIA. *(Shaking her head)* Not a trace.

RUBEK. Good, Then listen. — That day down there at the baths you said that you sensed I had become very nervous recently. —

MAIA. Yes, I was positive of that.

RUBEK. And what do you think the reason could be for *that*?

MAIA. How can I tell you—? *(Quickly)* Perhaps you had grown weary of this everlasting life together with me.

RUBEK. Everlasting—? Say rather: Eternal.

MAIA. Living together, day in and day out. We know how it was down there, we two solitary individuals, together four or five years and never more than an hour apart from each other. — We two always alone.

RUBEK. *(With interest)* Well, yes? What of that—?

MAIA. *(A bit depressed)* You are not a very sociable man, Rubek. You always keep to yourself and fight your battles alone. And I don't know how to talk properly to you of *your* affairs. All that about art and such things — *(Strikes out with her hand.)* And, God knows, I don't care for that matter!

RUBEK. Well, yes—yes; and that's why we just sat in front of the fire and prattled about *your* affairs.

MAIA. Oh, Good Lord, — I don't have any affairs to prattle about.

RUBEK. Well, they are trifles perhaps. But time passes for us in *that* way also, Maia.

MAIA. Yes, you are right. Time passes. You have observed that it is passing from you, Rubek! — And it is precisely *that* which makes you uneasy —

RUBEK. *(Nods vehemently)* And so restless! *(Twisting on the bench)* No, I cannot stand this miserable life much longer!

MAIA. *(Rises and stands a little while and looks at him.)* If you want to get rid of me, only say so.

RUBEK. Why must you use such language? Get rid of you?

MAIA. Yes, if you don't want me any longer, then speak right out. And I will go within the hour.

RUBEK. *(With an almost unnoticeable smile)* Is that intended as a threat, Maia?

MAIA. You know full well that what I said is no threat to you.

RUBEK. *(Rising)* No, you are right. *(After a pause)* You and I cannot possibly continue to live like this—

MAIA. Well, and therefore—!

RUBEK. There is no *therefore.* *(With emphasis on his words)* Because we can no longer live together *alone* — *that* does not mean that we must part.

MAIA. *(Smiling scornfully)* Only a little distance, you mean?

RUBEK. *(Shaking his head)* That's not needed either.

MAIA. Well then what? Come on: what do you plan to do with me?

RUBEK. *(Some hesitation)* What I now feel so keenly—and so painfully—is that I need to have someone with me who truly and willingly stands close—

MAIA. *(Interrupts him anxiously)* Don't *I* do that, Rubek?

RUBEK. *(Unwavering)* Not like I mean. I must live together with another person who can fulfill me, — complete me, — be *one* with me in all my actions.

MAIA. *(Slowly)* Yes, it is not easy for me to do that.

RUBEK. Oh no, you do not find that to your liking, Maia.

MAIA. *(Bursting out)* And, God knows, I get no pleasure from it, either!

RUBEK. That I know only too well. — And I was not thinking of finding a life helper when I married you.

MAIA. *(Studying him)* I see that you are thinking of another.

RUBEK. So? I never knew you to be a mind-reader. You can see *that*?

MAIA. Yes I can. Oh I understand you so well, so well, Rubek!

RUBEK. Well perhaps you can also see *whom* it is I am thinking about?

MAIA. Yes. I can do that easily.

RUBEK. Well? Who then—?

MAIA. You are thinking about that—that model you once employed to— *(Losing the train of thought)* Do you know that folks down at the hotel think she is mad?

RUBEK. Indeed? And what do the folks down at the hotel think about you and that bearslayer?

MAIA. That has nothing to do with it. *(Continuing the former idea)* But it was this pale lady you are thinking about.

RUBEK. *(Cheerfully)* Precisely of her. — When I no longer had employment for her—. And, besides that, she went away from me—vanished—without a word—

MAIA. Then you took me up as sort of a makeshift perhaps?

RUBEK. *(Even more unfeelingly)* Sort of that, to tell the truth, little Maia. I had for a year or a year and a half lived there lonely and brooding and had put the last—the very last touch to my work. "Resurrection Day" went out into the world and brought me fame—and everything else the heart desired. *(With more warmth)* But my heart was no longer in my work. The floral and incense offerings of mankind made me nauseated and I wanted to hide in the thickest woods. *(Looking at her)* You are a mindreader—can you guess what happened to me?

MAIA. *(Lightly)* Yes, you happened upon making portrait busts of gentlemen and ladies.

RUBEK. *(Nods)* On commission, yes. But with animal faces behind the masks. *That* I did gratis; no charge, you understand. *(Smiling)* But it was not exactly *that* I had in mind.

MAIA. What then?

RUBEK. *(Again seriously)* It was *this,* that everything about the artist's calling and the artist's mission—and such things, — began to appear to me to be empty and shallow and meaningless.

MAIA. What did you wish to put in its place?

RUBEK. Life, Maia.

MAIA. Life?

RUBEK. Yes, is not a life in sunshine and beauty far more valuable than one which drags to the end of its days in a foul, dank hole and toils till tired to death over clay lumps and stone blocks?

MAIA. *(With a little sigh)* Yes, I've always thought so.

RUBEK. Also I was now rich enough to live in luxury and idle in the quivering sunlight. I was able to build for myself the villa on Lake Taunitz and the mansion in the capital. And all those other things.

MAIA. *(Joining in his tone)* And so ultimately you were able to indulge yourself with me as well. And let me share in all your treasures.

RUBEK. *(Warding it off as a jest)* Didn't I promise to take you with me up on a high mountain and show you all the glories of the world?

MAIA. *(With a gentle expression)* Perhaps you have taken me with you up on a high enough mountain, Rubek, — but you have not shown me all the glories of the world.

RUBEK. *(Laughing irritatedly)* You are hard to please there, Maia! So very hard to please! *(Bursting out vehemently)* But do you know what I despair about most? Can you guess?

MAIA. *(With calm defiance)* Yes, it is just that now you are stuck with me—for your whole life.

RUBEK. I would not have expressed myself with such heartless words.

MAIA. But your meaning would have been just as heartless.

RUBEK. You have no understanding of an artist's nature and inner being.

MAIA. *(Smiling and shaking her head)* Good God, I don't even understand my own inner being.

RUBEK. *(Continuing undisturbed)* I live at such a fast pace, Maia. We live fast, we artists. I have lived through a whole lifetime in the few years we two have known each other. I now see that the happiness I seek cannot be found in idle niceties. Life lies not in that direction for me and my kind. I must go on working—creating work upon work—up until my last day. *(With an effort)* And for that reason I can no longer get along with you, Maia—No longer with you alone.

MAIA. *(Quietly)* You mean, to put it bluntly, that you are tired of me.

RUBEK. *(Bursting out)* Yes, I mean that! I have grown tired —unendurably tired and bored and listless from this life with you. Now you know. *(Controlling himself)* These are ugly, hard words I am using. I am aware of that. And I don't hold you guilty—I admit that willingly. It is only in me that this change has taken place. — *(Half to himself)* My awakening to what life really is.

MAIA. *(Involuntarily folding her hands)* Then why in the world can't we separate?

RUBEK. *(Looking at her in astonishment)* Would you be willing to do that?

MAIA. *(Shrugging her shoulders)* Oh yes—If there is nothing else—

RUBEK. *(Eagerly)* But there *is* something else. There *is* another way out—

MAIA. *(Holding up her forefinger)* You are thinking of the pale lady again!

RUBEK. Yes, in fact, I seem to have her on my mind constantly. Ever since I met her again. *(Stepping nearer)* I'll tell you a secret, Maia.

MAIA. Well?

RUBEK. *(Touching his breast)* In here, you see—in here I have a tiny pick-proof casket. And in that casket all my imaginary vision lies in custody. But when she went away without a trace, the casket lock closed. And she had the key. — And she took *that* with her. — You, little Maia, you had no key. Therefore all that it contains lies unused. And the years go by! I have no means of getting at the treasure.

MAIA. *(Trying to hide a subtle smile)* Then get her to unlock it for you again—

RUBEK. *(Not understanding)* Maia— ?

MAIA. —For here she is now. And it is no doubt on account of the casket that she has come.

RUBEK. I have not said a single word of this to her!

MAIA. *(Looking innocently at him)* My dear Rubek, — is it worth it to make all this fuss about something that is so obvious?

RUBEK. Do you think this matter is that obvious?

MAIA. Yes, I certainly do. Join the one who suits your needs. *(Nodding to him)* I can always manage to find a place for myself.

RUBEK. Where do you mean?

MAIA. *(Unconcerned, evasive)* Well—I could always get away to the villa if it becomes necessary. But it won't. Because in the city—in that great big house of ours, surely there must be—if we are all tolerant—there must be room for three.

RUBEK. *(Uncertainly)* And you think *that* would last for long?

MAIA. *(In a light tone)* Good Lord—if it doesn't then it doesn't, that's all. It's no good talking about it.

RUBEK. And what shall we do then, Maia—if it does *not* work?

MAIA. *(Unperturbed)* Then we simply get out of each other's way. Part completely. I can always find myself something new someplace in the world. Something free! Free! Free! — Don't worry about *that*, Professor Rubek! *(Pointing suddenly off to the right)* See *there!* There she is.

RUBEK. *(Turning)* Where?

MAIA. Out on the plain. Advancing—like a marble statue. She is coming this way.

RUBEK. *(Stands and gazes with hand over eyes)* Doesn't she look like the living image of resurrection? *(To himself)* And I tried to remove her—And cover her in shadows! Remodel her—I was a fool!

MAIA. What is *that* supposed to mean?

RUBEK. *(Avoiding her question)* Not a thing. Nothing that *you* would be able to understand.

(IRENE enters from the right over the uplands. The playing children have already caught sight of her and run to meet her. She is now surrounded by a flock of children; some seem free and confident, others shy and uneasy. She talks softly to them and indicates they must go down to the sanatorium; she herself will rest a while by the brook. The children jump down over the bank in the middle ground to the left. IRENE goes to the wall of rock and lets the streams of water flow coolingly over her hands.)

MAIA. *(Softly)* Go down and talk to her in private, Rubek.

RUBEK. And where will *you* go meanwhile?

MAIA. *(Looking meaningfully at him)* I go my own way from now on. *(She goes down from the hill and vaults over the brook with aid of her staff. She stops beside IRENE.)*

MAIA. Professor Rubek is up there waiting for you, Madam.

IRENE. What does he want?

MAIA. He wants you to help him with a casket which he is unable to unlock.

IRENE. Can I help him in that?

MAIA. He says you are the only one who can.

IRENE. Then I must try.

MAIA. You really must, Madam. *(She goes down the path to the sanatorium.)*

(After a while PROFESSOR RUBEK comes down to IRENE, but in such a way that the brook remains between them.)

IRENE. *(After a short pause)* She, the other one, said that you have been waiting for me.

RUBEK. I have waited for you year after year, — without realizing that.

IRENE. I could not come to you, Arnold. I lay down there sleeping the long, deep, dream-filled sleep.

RUBEK. But now you have awakened, Irene!

IRENE. *(Shaking her head)* I have the heavy, deep sleep on my eyelids yet.

RUBEK. You shall see, it will dawn and grow light for both of us.

IRENE. Don't trust that.

RUBEK. *(Urgently)* I have trust in that! And I know it! Now that I have found you again—

IRENE. Resurrected.

RUBEK. Transfigured!

IRENE. Only resurrected, Arnold. But not transfigured. *(He balances on the stones in the water and crosses to her.)*

RUBEK. Where have you been for the whole day, Irene?

IRENE. *(Pointing off)* Far, far away on the vast, dead land. —

RUBEK. *(Leading her on)* You don't have your—your friend with you today, I see.

IRENE. *(Smiling)* My friend keeps a good eye on me all the same.

RUBEK. Can she?

IRENE. *(Casting glances around)* You can trust in that. No matter where I am. She always has me in sight — *(Whispering)* Until I, one fine sunshiny day, put her to death.

RUBEK. Do you want that?

IRENE. With the greatest of pleasure. If only I were able to.

RUBEK. Why do you want it?

IRENE. Because she practices witchcraft. *(Mysterously)* Think of this, Arnold — She has transformed herself into my shadow.

RUBEK. *(Trying to calm her)* Well, well, well, — A shadow is something we all have.

IRENE. I am my own shadow. *(An ourburst)* Don't you understand that!

RUBEK. *(Depressed)* Yes, yes, Irene, — I understand that. *(He sits on a stone beside the brook. She stands behind him leaning on the rocky wall.)*

IRENE. *(After a bit)* Why do you sit there and turn your eyes from me?

RUBEK. *(Softly, shaking his head)* I dare not, — dare not look at you.

IRENE. Why don't you dare that any more?

RUBEK. You have a shadow that pains you. And *I* have my troubled conscience.

IRENE. *(With a joyous cry of freedom)* At last!

RUBEK. *(Jumping up)* Irene, — What is it!

IRENE. *(Motioning him away)* Only calm, calm, calm. *(Breathes heavily and says as though released from a burden)* There

now. Now they've let go of me. For the while. — Now we can
sit and talk together as before — when living.

RUBEK. Oh, if only we could talk as before

IRENE. Sit there where you sat. And I'll sit beside you. *(He
sits down again. She sits on another stone nearby.)*

IRENE. *(After a short silence)* Now I have come back to you
from the nethermost regions, Arnold.

RUBEK. Yes, truly, from an endlessly long journey.

IRENE. Come home to my Lord and Master—

RUBEK. To us — To what is ours alone, Irene.

IRENE. Have you waited for me every single day?

RUBEK. How could I dare to wait?

IRENE. *(With a sidelong glance)* No, you wouldn't dare. For
you understood nothing.

RUBEK. And it was not for the sake of another that you left
me?

IRENE. Couldn't it have been for *your* sake, Arnold?

RUBEK. *(Looking doubtfully at her)* I don't understand
you—?

IRENE. When I had served you with my soul and with my
body—and the statue stood completed—our child, as you
called it—then I laid at your feet the dearest offering of all
—I erased myself forever from your life.

RUBEK. *(Bowing his head)* And laid my life waste.

IRENE. *(Suddenly flaring up) That* is just what I wanted!
That you would never, never be able to create another thing
—after you had created our first child.

RUBEK. It was jealousy then?

IRENE. *(Coldly)* I think it was nearer to hatred.

RUBEK. Hatred? Hatred toward me?

IRENE. *(Again violently)* Yes, toward you—toward the artist, who completely without pity or concern took a warm-
blooded body, a young human life and tore the soul out of
it—because you needed it to create a work of art.

RUBEK. And *you* can say, that? — You, who brought the
radiant light of a sacred passion with you into my work? Into
that work which every morning joined us together, as if at
devotion.

IRENE. *(Coldly, as before)* Let me tell you one thing, Arnold.

RUBEK. Well?

IRENE. I never loved your art before I met you — Nor
afterwards, either.

RUBEK. But the artist, Irene?

IRENE. The artist I hate.

RUBEK. The artist in me also?

IRENE. Most of all in you. When I stripped myself completely and stood there before you, then I hated you, Arnold—

RUBEK. *(Warmly)* Surely you did not, Irene! That is not true.

IRENE. I hated you because you could stand there so unaffected—

RUBEK. *(Laughs)* Unaffected? You think so?

IRENE. —Or rather so irritatingly in control. And because you were an artist, only an artist—not a man! *(Changing to a warm, feeling tone.)* But that statue in the wet, living clay, *that* I loved—even as it stepped forth an animate human being out of the raw, formless mass—for *that* was *our* creation, *our* child. Mine and yours.

RUBEK. *(Sadly)* In spirit and in truth it was.

IRENE. I tell you, Arnold—it is for the sake of our child that I have taken upon myself this long pilgrimage.

RUBEK. *(Suddenly alert)* For a marble statue—?

IRENE. Call it what you will. I call it our child.

RUBEK. *(Uneasily)* And you wish to see it now? Completed? In marble, which you always felt to be so cold? *(Eagerly)* Perhaps you do not know it has been installed in a great museum somewhere—far out in the world?

IRENE. I have heard a sort of legend about it.

RUBEK. And museums were always abhorrent to you. You called them grave-vaults—

IRENE. I must make a pilgrimage to where my soul and my soul's child lie buried.

RUBEK. *(Anxious and uneasy)* You must never see the statue again! Do you hear, Irene! I entreat you—! Never, never see it again!

IRENE. Perhaps you think I will die again if I do?

RUBEK. *(Clasping hands)* Oh, I don't know what I think. How could I even imagine you were so attached to that statue? When you left me—before it was fully born.

IRENE. It was full-born. That is why I could go. And leave you alone.

RUBEK. *(Sits with his elbows on his knees, cradling his head with his hands over his eyes.)* It was not what it later became.

IRENE. *(Silently and with the speed of lightning she half-way unsheathes a thin, sharp knife from her breast and speaks in a hoarse whisper)* Arnold—have you done something evil to our child?

RUBEK. *(Evasively)* Something evil? — I cannot be certain what *you* will call it.

IRENE. *(Breathlessly)* Tell me straight out what you have done with the child!

RUBEK. I will tell you if you will sit and listen quietly to what I say.

IRENE. *(Hiding the knife)* I shall listen as quietly as a mother can when she—

RUBEK. *(Interrupting)* And you must not look at me while I am telling you this.

IRENE. *(Moving herself onto a stone behind his back)* I'll sit here behind your back. — Now tell me.

RUBEK. *(Taking his hands from his eyes and looking straight in front of himself)* When I had found you, I knew at once how I should employ you in my life's work.

IRENE. You called "Resurrection Day" your life's work— I called it "our child."

RUBEK. I was young then. Without any experience in life. I imagined resurrection in the form of a beautiful and delicate young woman—without any worldly experience—awakening to light and glory with no ugliness or impurity to shed.

IRENE. *(Quickly)* Yes—and isn't that how I stand there now?

RUBEK. *(Hesitating)* Not exactly in that form, Irene.

IRENE. *(With growing excitement)* Not exactly—? Not in the form I stood for you?

RUBEK. *(Without answering)* I became worldly wise in the years that followed, Irene. "Resurrection Day" became something more to me—something more all-encompassing in my understanding. The little round pedestal on which you stood so straight and solitary—it no longer had room enough for all that I wanted to compose—

IRENE. *(Searches for the knife, but lets it be)* What more did you compose? Tell me!

RUBEK. I added to the composition that which surrounded me in the world I saw with my own eyes. I had to include it. Could not help it, Irene. I widened the pedestal —it became grand and spacious; and on it I placed a portion of the curving, bursting earth. And up from ravines in the earth there now swarm human creatures with vaguely animal-like expressions. Women and men—just as I perceived them in life.

IRENE. *(In breathless suspense)* But in the middle of this swarm stands the young woman with the joy of light transforming her? — I still do that, Arnold?

RUBEK. *(Evasively)* Not exactly in the middle. Unfortunately, I had to transpose the statue back a little. For the sake of the overall effect, you understand. It would have dominated the whole too much otherwise.

IRENE. But the joy of light streams over my transfigured face as always?

RUBEK: That it does, Irene. For the most part. A bit subdued perhaps. In the manner which my altered ideas demanded.

IRENE. *(Rising noiselessly)* That design expresses the life you now see, Arnold.

RUBEK. Yes, I believe it does.

IRENE. And in that design you have shifted me back, faded out somewhat—as a background figure—within a group. *(She brings forth the knife.)*

RUBEK. Not a background figure. Let us at the most call it a middle-ground image—or some such.

IRENE. *(Whispering hoarsely)* You have just pronounced your own doom. *(About to strike.)*

RUBEK. *(Turns and looks up at her.)* Doom?

IRENE. *(Hastily hides the knife and says as though sick from pain)* My whole soul—you and I—we, we, we, and our child were in that solitary image.

RUBEK. *(Eagerly, removing his hat and wiping the sweat from his brow)* Yes, but let me tell you also how I have placed *myself* in the group. In front, beside a spring, like here, sits a guilt-burdened man unable to free himself from the earth's crust. I call him remorse for a wasted life. He sits there and dips his fingers in the running water—for he wants them clean—and he is gnawed and tortured by the knowledge that he never, never will succeed. He will never in all eternity be free to rise to a resurrected life. He will forever sit in this Hell.

IRENE. *(Hard and cold)* Poet!

RUBEK. Why poet?

IRENE. Because you are spoiled and foolish and only too

ready to forgive all your life's actions and all your life's thoughts. You have put my soul to death—and so you model yourself in remorse and penance and confession, — *(Smiling)* — and with that you think to settle your account.

RUBEK. *(Defiantly)* I am an artist, Irene. And I am not ashamed of whatever shortcomings I may have. But I was born an artist, you see—and will always remain an artist no matter what.

IRENE. *(Looks at him with a smile that seems to cover evil and says gently and softly)* You are a poet, Arnold. *(Softly stroking his hair)* You dear, great aging child—can't you see *that*?

RUBEK. *(Annoyed)* Why do you continue to call me poet?

IRENE. *(With a cunning look)* Because there is some forgiveness in that word, my friend. Some pardon for sins—it spreads a cape over all shortcomings. *(A sudden change of tone.)* But *I* was a human being—then! And *I* too had a life to live—and a human destiny to fulfill. And I let all of that go—gave it up in order to submit myself to you. And that was suicide. A deadly sin against my own self. *(Half whispering)* And that is a sin I can never make amends for. *(She seats herself near him by the brook, keeps close watch on him with her eyes and almost absent-mindedly plucks some flowers from the shrubbery around them.)*
(With outward self-control) I should have borne children into the world. Many children. Real children. Not the kind that lie hidden in grave vaults. That was my calling. I should never have served you, Poet.

RUBEK. *(Lost in remembrance)* Those *were* beautiful times, Irene. Marvelously beautiful times, when I think back—

IRENE. *(Looks at him with a tender expression)* Can you remember a little word you said—when you had finished—finished with me and with our child? *(Nodding to him)* Can you remember that little word, Arnold?

RUBEK. *(Looking inquiringly at her)* Did I say something in particular that you still remember?

IRENE. Yes, you did. Can't you remember?

RUBEK. *(Shaking his head)* No, I can't say I do. Not this instant at any rate.

IRENE. You took both my hands and pressed them warmly. And I stood there in breathless anticipation. And then you said: "I must offer you my heart-felt thanks, Irene. This," you said, "has been a fortunate episode for me."

RUBEK. *(Looks up unbelievingly)* I said "episode"? I don't ordinarily use that word.

IRENE. You said "episode."

RUBEK. *(With fake cheerfulness)* Oh, well—After all that's what it *was* really, an episode.

IRENE. *(Curtly)* At *that* word I left you.

RUBEK. You take everything so painfully deep, Irene.

IRENE. *(Rubbing her forehead)* You are right there. Let us rid ourselves of all that depth and weight. *(Plucking the petals from a mountain rose and sprinkling them on the brook)* Look there, Arnold. There swim our birds.

RUBEK. What manner of birds are they?

IRENE. Can't you see? They are flamingos. For they are rose-red.

RUBEK. Flamingos don't swim. They only wade.

IRENE. So they are not flamingos then. They are gulls.

RUBEK. Yes, they could be gulls with red beaks. *(Plucking broad green leaves and casting them out)* Now I send my ships out after them.

IRENE. But there must be no harpoon-men aboard.

RUBEK. No, there shall be no harpoon-men. *(Smiling at her)* Can you recall the summer we sat like this in front of that little cottage on Lake Taunitz?

IRENE. *(Nodding)* Saturday evenings, yes—when we were finished with our work for the week—

RUBEK. —and traveled out there by rail. And stayed there over Sunday—

IRENE. *(With an evil, hate-filled gleam in her eyes)* That was an episode, Arnold.

RUBEK. *(As though he did not hear)* In those times you also set birds swimming in the brook. They were water-lillies, which you—

IRENE. White swans they were.

RUBEK. I meant swans, yes. And I recall that I fastened a great, downy leaf to one of the swans. It looked like a thistle—

IRENE. Then it became Lohengrin's boat—drawn by a swan.

RUBEK. How happy that game made you, Irene.

IRENE. We played it over and over again.

RUBEK. Every single Saturday, I think. The whole summer long.

IRENE. You said I was the swan that drew your boat.

RUBEK. I said that? Yes, that could be. *(Absorbed in the game)* Now see how the gulls are swimming down the river.

IRENE. *(Laughing)* And all your ships are stranded.

RUBEK. *(Throwing more leaves in the brook)* I have many ships in reserve. *(Following the leaves with his eyes, sprinkles out more leaves and says after a moment)* Dearest Irene—I have bought that little cottage on Lake Taunitz.

IRENE. You have bought it? You often said that you would buy it if you had the money.

RUBEK. Since then I came by the money. And so I bought it.

IRENE. *(Sidelong glance at him)* Then you live out there—in our old house?

RUBEK. No, I had that torn down long ago. And then I built for myself a great, impressive, commodious villa on the site—with an encircling park. *There* it is our custom— *(Stops and corrects himself)* *There* I customarily stay during the summers—

IRENE. *(Controlling herself)* Then you and—and the other one stay there now?

RUBEK. *(A bit defiantly)* Yes, if my wife and I are not traveling—as we are now.

IRENE. *(Looking far off)* The life at Lake Taunitz was beautiful.

RUBEK. *(As though looking back into himself)* And nevertheless, Irene—

IRENE. *(Completing his thought)* —Nevertheless we let all the beauty of that life slip away.

RUBEK. *(Softly, urgently)* Is it *too* late for repentance now?

IRENE. *(Does not answer him, but sits silently for a moment; then points out over the plain.)* Look, Arnold. The sun is sinking behind the peaks. Just look—how the red glow slants down over the heathery slopes out there.

RUBEK. *(Looks where she points)* It has been a long time since I have seen a mountain sunset.

IRENE. Or a sunrise either?

RUBEK. I don't think I have ever seen a sunrise.

IRENE. *(Smiles as though lost in a remembrance.)* I once saw a wonderfully beautiful sunrise.

RUBEK. You did? Where was that?

IRENE. High, high up on a dizzy mountaintop. — You fooled me into going up there by promising that I should be able to see all the world's glories if only I — *(She stops suddenly)*

RUBEK. If only you—? Well?

IRENE. I did as you told me. Followed you up to the heights. And there fell on my knees—and worshipped you. And served you. *(Silent a moment; then she says softly)* Then I saw the sunrise.

RUBEK. *(Changing)* Wouldn't you like to come along and stay with us in the villa down there?

IRENE. *(Smiling scornfully at him)* Together with you—and the other woman?

RUBEK. *(Urgently)* Together with *me*—like those creative days. Open up all that is twisted and locked within me. Don't you want to do that, Irene?

IRENE. *(Shaking her head)* I no longer have the key to you, Arnold.

RUBEK. You *have* the key! You alone have it! *(Begging her)* Help me—that I may live my life over again!

IRENE. *(Unmoved as before)* Hollow dreams. Wasted—dead dreams. *Our* life together there can have no resurrection.

RUBEK. *(Curtly, breaking off)* Then let us go on playing!

IRENE. Yes play—only play! *(They sit and scatter leaves and petals out over the brook where they swim and sail along.)*

(Up the slope to the left in the background ULFHEIM *and* MAIA *enter in hunting clothes. After them follows the* SERVANT *with the hounds, with which he exits to the right.)*

RUBEK. *(Seeing them)* Look, there goes little Maia off with the bear shooter.

IRENE. Your lady, yes.

RUBEK. Or else the other's.

MAIA. *(Looking around from the upland, seeing the two by the brook, she calls out.)* Good night, Professor! Dream of me. Now I go forth on an adventure.

RUBEK. *(Calling back)* What is your quest?

MAIA. *(Coming nearer)* To put *living* in place of everything else.

RUBEK. *(Mocking)* *You* also want that, little Maia?

MAIA. Oh yes. I've made up a song about it: *(Singing jubilantly)*

I am free! I am free! I am free!
Far beyond life's prison I see!
Like the flight of a bird I am free!
For I know, yes, I know I've awakened at last
—finally.

RUBEK. It seems you have.

MAIA. *(Breathing a deep breath)* Oh, — How divine, how weightless I feel to wake up at last!

RUBEK. Good night, Mrs. Maia—and luck until—

ULFHEIM. *(Calling out in interruption)* Shut up! Give the devil your evil wishes. Can't you see we are going out to shoot—

RUBEK. What will you bring me home from the hunt, Maia?

MAIA. You shall have a bird of prey, which you can use as a model. I'll wing one for you.

RUBEK. *(Laughs mockingly and bitterly)* Yes, wing-shots—all unaware—that has always been your way.

MAIA. *(Tossing her head)* Oh, I can shift for myself if I must. *(Nodding and laughing roguishly)* So farewell—and have a nice, peaceful summer night on the uplands!

RUBEK. *(Jesting)* Thank you! And all the bad luck in the world to you both and your hunt!

ULFHEIM. *(Laughing uproariously)* Now *that* is a wish as it *should* be!

MAIA. *(Also laughing)* Thanks, thanks, thanks, Professor! *(They have both crossed over what can be seen of the uplands and exit through the bushes to the right.)*

RUBEK. *(After a short pause)* Summer night on the uplands. *That's* what life should be.

IRENE. *(Suddenly, with a wild look in her eyes)* Do you *desire* a summer night on the uplands—with me?

RUBEK. *(Stretching out his arms)* Yes, yes—Come!

IRENE. You, my beloved lord and master!

RUBEK. Oh, Irene!

IRENE. *(Hoarsely, smiling and groping in her breast)* It will be but an episode— *(Quickly, whispering)* Hush—Don't look round, Arnold!

RUBEK. *(Also low-voiced)* What is it?

IRENE. A face there staring at me.

RUBEK. *(Turning involuntarily)* Where? *(With a start)* Ah—!

(The DEACONESS *'s head has come half way into sight among the bushes by the slope descending to the left. Her eyes are immovably fixed on* IRENE.*)*

IRENE. *(Rises and says softly)* Then we must part. No, you must remain seated. Do you hear? You must not follow me. *(Bends over him and whispers)* Till we meet tonight. On the uplands.

RUBEK. You will come, Irene?

IRENE. Yes, surely I will come. Wait for me here.

RUBEK. *(Repeating dreamily)* Summer night on the uplands. With you. With you. *(His eyes meet hers.)* Oh, Irene—that's what life could have been—And we have lost that, we two.

IRENE. We only see what is beyond recovery when— *(Breaking off short)*

RUBEK. *(Looking inquiringly at her)* When—!

IRENE. When we dead awaken.

RUBEK. (Shaking his head sadly) Yes, what can we see really?

IRENE. We can see that we have never lived. *(She goes over the slope and disappears. The* DEACONESS *makes way for her and follows after.)*

*(*PROFESSOR RUBEK *remains sitting motionless by the brook.)*

MAIA. *(Heard singing jubilantly up among the mountains)*

> I am free! I am free! I am free!
> Far beyond life's prison I see
> Like the flight of a bird I am free!

Third Act

(A wild, crevassed mountain slope with steep cliffs for a back drop. Snow-clad peaks rise to the right and are lost in driving mist higher up. To the left, on a stone outcrop, is an old, half-fallen hut. It is early morning. Dawn is breaking. The sun is not yet up.

MAIA *enters, blushing red with irritation, over the outcropping to the left.* ULFHEIM *follows, half angry, half laughing, and holding her fast by the sleeve.)*

MAIA. *(Trying to tear herself loose)* Let me go! Let me go, I say!

ULFHEIM. Oh, no—I'm not afraid of your bite. But you're as temperamental as a wolverine.

MAIA. *(Striking his hands)* Let me go, I say! And behave yourself—

ULFHEIM. No, I won't do that either.

MAIA. Then I won't go another step with you. You hear —not a single step—!

ULFHEIM. Ho-ho—How can you escape from me here on the wild mountain side?

MAIA. I'll jump over the cliff there if I have to—

ULFHEIM. And mash and mangle yourself up into dog-food—a nice bloody morsel. *(Releases her hand.)* Go ahead. Jump over the cliff now if that is your wish. It's a dizzy height. Only one narrow footpath down and that next to impassable.

MAIA. *(Brushing her skirt with her hands and looking at him with angry eyes)* Sure. Aren't you a nice one to go on a hunt with!

ULFHEIM. Don't you mean: to go sporting with?

MAIA. Oh, so you call this sport do you?

ULFHEIM. Yes, if I may be so bold—this is the sport I like best.

MAIA. *(Tossing her head)* Well—I must say! *(After a moment; looks searchingly at him.)* Why did you let the dogs loose up there?

ULFHEIM. *(Winking and smiling)* So that *they* also might do a little hunting of their own, do you know what I mean?

MAIA. That's not true at all! It wasn't for the dog's sake that you let them go.

ULFHEIM. *(Still smiling)* Well, why did I? Let's hear—?

MAIA. You loosed them because you wanted to get rid of Lars. He had to run after them and leash them again, you said. And in the meantime—. Well aren't you a fine one!

ULFHEIM. —In the meantime—?

MAIA. *(Curtly breaking off)* Never mind.

ULFHEIM. *(In a confidential tone)* Lars won't find them. You can take an oath on that. He won't come back with them until the time is up.

MAIA. *(Looking angrily at him)* No, I'm sure he won't.

ULFHEIM. *(Grasping for her arm)* Because Lars—he knows my—my sporting ways, you see.

MAIA. *(Eluding him and measuring him with a glance)* Do you know what you look like, Mr. Ulfheim?

ULFHEIM. I just look like my own self, I'm well aware of that.

MAIA. Yes, that's true. But you are the living image of a faun.

ULFHEIM. A faun—?

MAIA. Yes, exactly, a faun.

ULFHEIM. A faun. — Isn't that a sort of monster? Or sort of a wood-demon, you might say?

MAIA. Yes, you are just such a thing. A thing with the beard of a goat and the legs of a ram. Yes, and the faun has horns also!

ULFHEIM. Aha! — Has *he* horns as well?

MAIA. A pair of disgusting horns like you, yes.

ULFHEIM. Can you see the wretched horns *I* have grown?

MAIA. Yes, quite clearly.

ULFHEIM. *(Taking the dogs' leash out of his pocket)* Then I'd better tie you up.

MAIA. Are you crazy! You want to tie me up—?

ULFHEIM. I *look* like a devil, then I'll *be* a devil. Indeed! So you see horns, do you!

MAIA. *(Soothingly)* Now, now, now—behave yourself, Mr. Ulfheim. *(Breaking off)* But where is your hunting castle, the one you bragged so boldly about? It must be somewhere near here according to you.

ULFHEIM. *(Points with a flourish to the hut.)* Here it is before your very eyes.

MAIA. *(Looking at him)* That old pigsty?

ULFHEIM. *(Laughing in his beard)* It has housed more than *one* king's daughter.

MAIA. That is where the princess met the dreadful man disguised like a bear, as you told me?

ULFHEIM. Yes, fair hunting companion—this is the spot. *(With an inviting gesture of the hand)* Now if you would step inside, then—

MAIA. Ugh! I'll not set a foot in there — Ugh!

ULFHEIM. Oh, two people can doze away a summer night very pleasantly in there. Or a whole summer—as it may be.

MAIA. Thanks! That would take a strong stomach. *(Impatiently)* But I'm tired of both you and your hunt. I want to go down to the hotel now—before the folks wake up down there.

ULFHEIM. How do you think you will get there from here?

MAIA. That's your problem. I suppose there is some way or other to get down.

ULFHEIM. *(Points towards background)* Very well; something that serves well enough—right down the cliff over there—

MAIA. Just you watch—. If I really have to, then—

ULFHEIM. —Go ahead, test yourself and see if you dare go down that way.

MAIA. *(Doubtful)* You think I can't?

ULFHEIM. Never in the world. Not unless you get help from me—

MAIA. *(Uneasily)* Well then come and help me! What else are you here for?

ULFHEIM. Would you rather I take you on my back—

MAIA. Don't be silly!

ULFHEIM. — Or bear you in my arms?

MAIA. Stop talking such nonsense.

ULFHEIM. *(With suppressed resentment)* Once I took a young wench—lifted her up from the gutter and bore her in my arms. Single-handed I bore her. And wanted to bear her *this* way all through life; — so that she might not bruise her foot on a stone. For she had worn her shoes very thin when I found her—

MAIA. And in spite of that you took her up and bore her single-handed?

ULFHEIM. Took her up from the filth and bore her as high and gently as I could. *(With a growling laugh)* And do you know what thanks I got for that?

MAIA. No. What did you get?

ULFHEIM. *(Looking at her, smiling, and nodding)* I got horns. Horns which *you* can see so plainly. — Isn't that an amusing story, Madam Bear-Murderess?

MAIA. Oh, yes; very amusing. But I know another story which is even more amusing.

ULFHEIM. What is your *story* then?

MAIA. It is this. Once upon a time there was a stupid little girl who had both father and mother. But they were very poor. Then came a great and powerful Lord in among all this poverty. And he took the child up in his arms—as you did—and traveled far, far away with her—

ULFHEIM. Did she want so strongly to be with him?

MAIA. Yes, for she was stupid, you see.

ULFHEIM. And no doubt he was a very handsome man?

MAIA. Oh no, he was not in the least attractive. But he got her to believe that he would take her with him up on the highest mountain, where everything is covered with light and sunshine.

ULFHEIM. So he was a mountain climber, was he, this man?

MAIA. Yes, he was—in a way.

ULFHEIM. So he took the little girl up with him—?

MAIA. *(Tossing her head)* Sure — he really took her; you can bet! Oh, no, he duped her into a cold, damp cave, where there was no sun or fresh air—it seemed to *her*—even though the walls were gilded and lined with great, petrified ghosts.

ULFHEIM. Devil take me, that's what she deserved!

MAIA. Yes, but don't you think it's a very amusing story all the same?

ULFHEIM. *(Looking at her a moment)* Listen to me, my good hunting companion—

MAIA. Well? What now?

ULFHEIM. Why can't we stitch together our tattered fates?

MAIA. Would a gentleman stoop to becoming a mender of old clothes?

ULFHEIM. Yes, I will. We two could try to patch the tatters here and there,—in order to piece together a human life out of them.

MAIA. And if these same tatters are worn too thin—what then?

ULFHEIM. *(Striking out with his hand)* Then we will be exposed to view in those places, but so what—that's what we really are!

MAIA. *(Laughs)* You with your goats' legs, yes!

ULFHEIM. And you with your—. Well, let that go.

MAIA. Yes, come, — let *us* go.

ULFHEIM. Stop! Where to, Comrade?

MAIA. Down to the hotel, of course.

ULFHEIM. And after that?

MAIA. Then we say farewell to each other and thanks for the company.

ULFHEIM. Can *we* separate, we two? Do you think we *can* do that?

MAIA. Yes, you were not able to tie me up, you know.

ULFHEIM. I have a castle to give you—

MAIA. *(Pointing at the hut)* A *match* for that one?

ULFHEIM. It hasn't tumbled down yet.

MAIA. And perhaps all the glories of the world?

ULFHEIM. A castle, I said—

MAIA. Thanks! I've had enough of castles.

ULFHEIM. —with splendid hunting grounds circling round it for miles.

MAIA. Are there works of art in this castle also?

ULFHEIM. *(Slowly)* No—there are really no works of art; but—

MAIA. *(Relieved)* Ah, that's one good thing!

ULFHEIM. Then you will go with me—as far and as long as I demand?

MAIA. There is a tame bird of prey who sits watch over me.

ULFHEIM. *(Wildly)* We'll put a bullet in his wing, Maia!

MAIA. *(Looks a moment at him and says determinedly)* Then come and carry me down into the depths.

ULFHEIM. *(Throwing his arms around her waist)* It's high time! The mist is covering us—!

MAIA. Is the way down terribly hazardous?

ULFHEIM. The mountain mist is more hazardous. *(She shakes herself loose, goes to the edge of the cliff and looks over, but starts back at once.)*

ULFHEIM. *(Goes to meet her and laughs.)* Well, a bit dizzy are you?

MAIA. *(Faintly)* Yes, *that* too. But go over and look down. There are two climbing—

ULFHEIM. *(Goes and bends over the mountain edge.)* It is only your bird of prey—and his strange lady.

MAIA. Can't we slip by them—without their seeing us?

ULFHEIM. Impossible. The trail is much too narrow. And it's the only way down from here.

MAIA. *(Mustering her composure)* All right— Then we'll confront them here!

ULFHEIM. Spoken like a true bearslayer, Comrade!

(PROFESSOR RUBEK and IRENE come into view over the precipice in the background. He has his plaid over his shoulders, she has a fur cape thrown loosely over her dress and a swansdown hood over her head.)

RUBEK. *(Still only half visible over the cliff edge)* Well, Maia! So we two meet once more?

MAIA. *(With posed coolness)* Your servant. Please, come up.

(PROFESSOR RUBEK climbs all the way up and reaches a hand for IRENE, who also comes up onto the level.)

RUBEK. *(Coldly to his wife)* You have been together on the mountain all night? You two—as we have?

MAIA. I have been on a hunt—yes. You gave me your permission.

ULFHEIM. *(Pointing into the depths)* You came up by that pathway?

RUBEK. As you saw, yes.

ULFHEIM. The strange lady also?

RUBEK. Yes, of course. *(With a glance at MAIA)* The strange lady and I intend never to part ways again.

ULFHEIM. It is a deadly way you have come, you know?

RUBEK. Nonetheless we tried it. Because it was not very bad at the beginning.

ULFHEIM. No, at the beginning nothing seems bad. But then one can come to a tight place where one can neither go forward nor back. And so one is stuck fast, Mr. Professor! Mountain-fast, we hunters call it.

RUBEK. *(Smiles and says to him)* Are you trying to give advice to me, sir?

ULFHEIM. God help me, I'm no wise man. *(Urgently, pointing up to the heights)* But can't you see the storm is closing in on us? Hear the wind rising?

RUBEK. *(Listening)* It sounds like the prelude to the Day of Resurrection.

ULFHEIM. It's the storm gust from the peaks, man! See those clouds dropping down. They'll wrap around us like a shroud.

IRENE. *(Cowering)* I know that shroud.

MAIA. *(Drawing* ULFHEIM *aside)* Let's hurry down.

ULFHEIM. *(To the* PROFESSOR*)* I can't help more than *one.* Stay in the hut for now—while the storm rages. Then I'll send folks up to fetch the both of you.

IRENE. *(In terror)* To fetch us! No, No—!

ULFHEIM. *(Harshly)* By force if it comes to that. For that stands between life and death here. Now you know. *(To* MAIA*)* Come then. — You will have to trust my strength.

MAIA. *(Clinging to him)* Oh, how I shall rejoice and sing if I get down unharmed!

ULFHEIM. *(Begins to descend and calls to the others.)* Wait there in the hunting lodge till the men come with ropes to fetch you.

*(*ULFHEIM, *with* MAIA *in his arms, scrambles rapidly and carefully down into the depths.)*

IRENE. *(Looks for some time with terror-filled eyes at* PROFESSOR RUBEK.*)* Did you hear that, Arnold? — Men will come up and fetch me! Many men will come up here—!

RUBEK. Be calm, Irene!

IRENE. *(In growing fear)* And she, the one clad in black— she will come too. For she will have missed me long since. And then she will take hold of me, Arnold! And put me in a straitjacket. Yes, she has one with her in a case. I have seen it—

RUBEK. No human being shall be allowed to touch you.

IRENE. *(With a wild smile)* Oh, no—I have my own means against that.

RUBEK. What means?

IRENE. *(Drawing forth the knife)* This!

RUBEK. *(Grabbing for it)* You have a knife—!

IRENE. Always, always. Both day and night. In bed also.

RUBEK. Give me the knife, Irene!

IRENE. *(Hiding it)* You can't have it. I may very well find a use of my own.

RUBEK. What use can you find here?

IRENE. *(Looking hard at him)* It was destined for *you,* Arnold.

RUBEK. For *me*!

IRENE. As we sat by the shore of Lake Taunitz last night—

RUBEK. By Taunitz—?

IRENE. In front of the cottage. And played with swans and water-lilies—

RUBEK. What then, — what then?

IRENE. —and then I heard you say with such icy, grave-coldness—that I was only an episode in your life—

RUBEK. It was *you* who said *that,* Irene! Not I.

IRENE. *(Continuing)* — so I brought forth the knife. For I wanted to thrust it into your back.

RUBEK. *(Darkly)* And why didn't you?

IRENE. Because it was then terrifyingly clear to me that you were dead already—had long been.

RUBEK. Dead?

IRENE. Dead. Dead, as I am. We sat by Lake Taunitz, we two cold corpses—and played together.

RUBEK. I don't call that dead. But you don't understand me.

IRENE. Where is that burning desire for me that you fought and struggled with when I stood freely before you as the resurrected woman?

RUBEK. Our love is surely not dead, Irene.

IRENE. That love is of this earthly life—this beautiful, wondrous earthly life—this enigmatic earthly life—which is dead in us both.

RUBEK. *(Passionately)* I tell you that same love—it seethes and burns within me as warmly as ever before!

IRENE. And I? Have you forgotten who I am now?

RUBEK. Be for me whatever you wish! You are to me the woman I see in dreams.

IRENE. I have posed on a turntable—naked—and shown myself freely to many hundreds of men—after you.

RUBEK. It was I who drove you to the turntable—blind as I once was! I who placed that dead clay image above life's —above love's happiness.

IRENE. *(Looks down)* Too late. Too late.

RUBEK. All that lies between has not by so much as a hair's breadth lowered you in my eyes.

IRENE. *(With head erect)* Nor in mine.

RUBEK. Well then! Then we are free. And there is still enough time for us to live life, Irene.

IRENE. *(Looking sadly at him)* The desire for life is dead in me, Arnold. Now that I am resurrected. I sought after you. And found you—and now I see that you and life lie dead—as I have lain.

RUBEK. Oh, how you have lost your way! Life in us and around us ferments and froths as before!

IRENE. *(Smiling and shaking her head)* The young resurrected woman can see the whole of life laid out on its death-bed.

RUBEK. *(Throwing his arms forcibly around her)* Then let us two dead for once live life to the dregs before we go down to our graves again!

IRENE. *(With a shriek)* Arnold!

RUBEK. But not here half in darkness! Not here where this ugly, wet shroud flaps around us—

IRENE. *(Transported by passion)* No, no—up in the light and in all the glittering glory. Up to the promised peak!

RUBEK. Up there we will celebrate our wedding, Irene—Oh my beloved!

IRENE. *(Proudly)* We will let the sun look upon us, Arnold.

RUBEK. Let all the powers of light look upon us. And all of darkness, too. *(Grasps her hand.)* Will you follow me, my redeemed bride?

IRENE. *(As though transfigured)* I willingly follow and serve my lord and master!

RUBEK. *(Drawing her with him)* First we must pass through the mists, Irene, and then—

IRENE. Yes, through all the mists. And then all the way up to the peak of the tower that shines in the sunrise.

(Mist clouds sink over the landscape. PROFESSOR RUBEK *with* IRENE *by the hand climbs up over the glacier to the right and soon disappears in the low clouds. Great storm-gusts chase and whirl through the air.)*

(The DEACONESS *enters from the stone ledge to the left. She stands there and looks silently and searchingly around.)*

MAIA. *(Heard jubilantly singing down in the depths)*

I am free! I am free! I am free!
Far beyond life's prison I see!
Like the flight of a bird I am free!

(Suddenly a thunderous roar is heard far up on the glacier. It slides and whirls downward with raging momentum. PROFESSOR RUBEK *and* IRENE *are glimpsed briefly in the midst of the avalanche which buries them.)*

DEACONESS. *(Lets out a shriek, stretches her arms towards where they fell, and cries)* Irene! *(Stands silent a moment, then she makes the sign of the cross before her in the air and says)* Pax vobiscum!

(MAIA *'s jubilant song sounds still farther down in the depths.)*

bibliography

Henrik Ibsen

Downs, Brian. *Ibsen: The Intellectual Background.* 1946.
Ibsen, Henrik. *Letters and Speeches,* ed. by Evert Spinchorn. 1964.
Koht, Halvdan. *The Life of Ibsen.* 1931.
Meyer, Michael. *Ibsen: A Biography.* 1971.
Northam, John. *Ibsen's Dramatic Method.* 1953.
Shaw, G. Bernard. *The Quintessence of Ibsenism.* 1913.
Tennant, P. F. *Ibsen's Dramatic Technique.* 1948.
Weigand, Hermann. *The Modern Ibsen.* 1925.

August Strindberg

Dahlstrom, C. E. W. L. *Strindberg's Dramatic Expressionism.* 1930.
McGill, V. J. *August Strindberg: The Bedeviled Viking.* 1930.
Mortenson, Brita, and Downs, Brian. *Strindberg.* 1949.
Sprigge, Elizabeth. *The Strange Life of August Strindberg.* 1949.
Strindberg, August. *Open Letters to the Intimate Theater.* 1955.

General

Bentley, Eric. *The Playwright as Thinker.* 1946.
Brockett, Oscar G., and Findlay, Robert R. *Century of Innovation.* 1973.
Lucas, F. L. *The Drama of Ibsen and Strindberg.* 1962.
Valency, Maurice. *The Flower and the Castle.* 1963.
Williams, Raymond. *Drama from Ibsen to Eliot.* 1952.

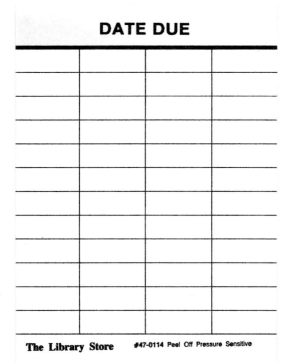

DATE DUE

The Library Store   #47-0114 Peel Off Pressure Sensitive